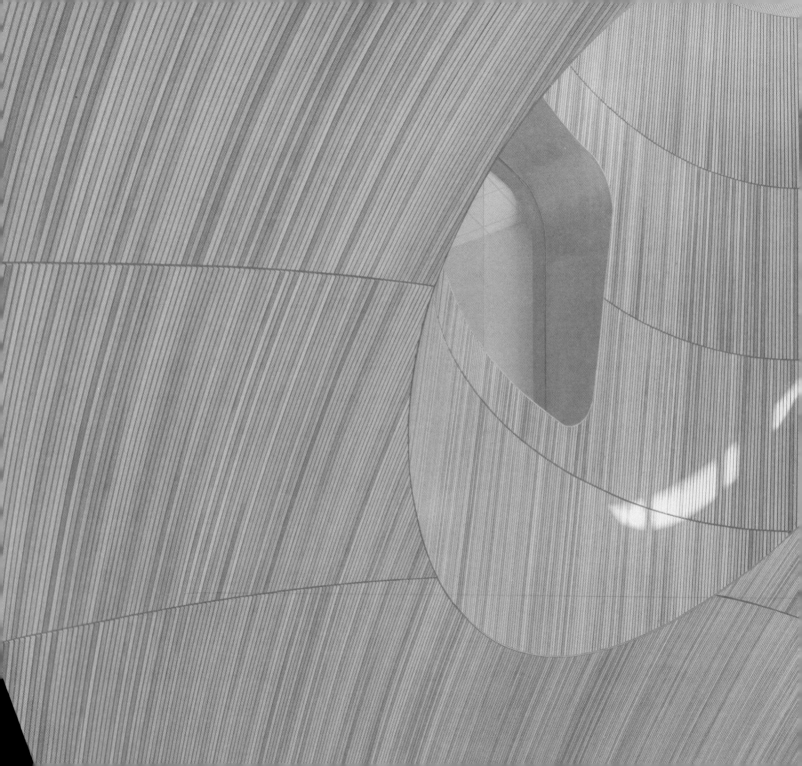

Library as Stoa

ORO Editions
Publishers of Architecture, Art, and Design
Gordon Goff: Publisher

www.oroeditions.com
info@oroeditions.com

Published by ORO Editions

Project Coordinator: Kirby Anderson
Book Design: Pablo Mandel @circularstudio
Typeset in Akzidenz-Grotesk and Plantin

10 9 8 7 6 5 4 3 2 1 First Edition

Library of Congress data available upon request. World Rights: Available

ISBN: 978-1-943532-22-3

Color Separations and Printing: ORO Group Ltd.
Printed in China.

International Distribution: www.oroeditions.com/distribution

ORO Editions makes a continuous effort to minimize the overall carbon footprint of its publications. As part of this goal,
ORO Editions, in association with Global ReLeaf, arranges to plant trees to replace those used in the manufacturing of the
paper produced for its books. Global ReLeaf is an international campaign run by American Forests, one of the world's oldest
nonprofit conservation organizations. Global ReLeaf is American Forests' education and action program that helps individuals,
organizations, agencies, and corporations improve the local and global environment by planting and caring for trees.

Library as Stoa

*Snøhetta, Public Space and Academic
Mission in The Charles Library*

Temple University,
Kate Wingert-Playdon with
Phillip M. Crosby

ORO

ORO Editions — Novato, California

Contents

Preface

Library as Stoa is based on a four-part symposium series, Building the 21st Century Library that was carried out between 2015 and 2018. The series was a collaboration between Temple Libraries and the Tyler School of Art and Architecture. The series had a straightforward premise. The Charles Library, valued both in terms of its function as a library and as a work of urban architecture, presented an opportunity for dialogue between professionals from cultural institutions and from built environment design disciplines. A main goal was to examine the relationship between architectural design and institutional intentions.

The dialogue ran in parallel to the design and building process for the Charles Library. It served as a venue for Temple's community to frame the importance of the Charles Library as a part of the University identity, guiding us into the future. Interesting discourse came from questions about cultural memory and architecture, social space and community, the relationship of campus and city, and access and opportunity as a campus infrastructure transforms.

The events were organized by Nicole Restaino and Sara Curnow Wilson, of Temple Libraries, guided by Margaret Carney, Joe Lucia, and Kate Wingert-Playdon. The range of voices from the Temple University and Philadelphia communities provided us with thoughtful insights about the role of social space and civic functions, prompting important thoughts about innovation and the future of cultural memory in the institutional setting. Questions from students and community members during the symposia were as important in providing insights as the responses of the panelists and are included as part of the narrative in the three essays in this book, *Social and Cultural Memory: The Idea of Library; Community and Cultural Identity: Stories, Spaces, Functions;* and *Civic Infrastructure: Campus, City, Culture.* Insights about the network of cultural institutions in Philadelphia—the Philadelphia Free Library, the Philadelphia Museum of Art, the Penn Libraries at the University of Pennsylvania, the Francis A. Drexel Library at St. Joseph's University, and the Athenaeum of Philadelphia—provided good comparative models from which to see the Charles Library's attributes. Insights about architecture and urban design from those who shape our environment through their practices gave context to the dialogue.

The design and construction of the Charles Library has had a positive impact on the Temple campus and will continue to have a positive impact on the Temple community. At the first symposium in February 2015, there was interesting dialogue about the role of the library as an institutional change agent. We will continue to witness its impact in terms of physical infrastructure, research innovation, and social identity for Temple University in the years to come.

Building the 21st Century Library
Symposium Series Participants

Architecture and the Evolution of the 21st Century Cultural Memory Institution
February 10, 2015

MODERATOR   Kate Wingert-Playdon, Associate Dean and Director of Architecture and Environmental Design, Tyler School of Art and Architecture
PANELISTS   Bruce Laverty, Curator of Architecture, The Athenaeum of Philadelphia
Joe Lucia, Dean, University Libraries, Temple University
William Noel, Director of the Kislak Center and the Schoenberg Institute for Manuscript Studies, University of Pennsylvania
Fon Wang, Director of Historic Preservation, Ballinger Architects

Campus, City, Culture
March 6, 2016

MODERATOR   Inga Saffron, Architecture Critic, The Philadelphia Inquirer
PANELISTS   Margaret Carney, University Architect, Temple University
Peter Conn, Executive Director, The Athenaeum of Philadelphia
Craig Dykers, Founding Partner, Snøhetta
Anne Fadullon, Director of the Department of Planning and Development, City of Philadelphia
Timothy Rub, George D. Widener Director and Chief Executive Officer, The Philadelphia Museum of Art

Stories, Spaces, Functions
April 4, 2017

MODERATORS   Emily Logan, Graduate Student, Fox School of Business
Arash Jafarian, Graduate Student, Tyler School of Art and Architecture
PANELISTS   Joe Benford, Deputy Director of Customer Engagement, The Free Library of Philadelphia
Elliot Felix, Founder and CEO, brightspot strategy
Joe Lucia, Dean, University Libraries, Temple University
Nathan McRae, Director, Senior Architect, Snøhetta

Transformation of a Campus
October 10, 2018

MODERATOR   Kevin J. Delaney, Vice Provost for Faculty Affairs, Temple University
PANELISTS   Karen Blanchard, Principal, SITIO Architecture + Urbanism
Dozie Ibeh, Associate Vice President, Project Delivery Group, Planning and Capital Projects, Temple University
Anne Krakow, Library Director, St. Joseph's University
Siobhan Reardon, President and Director, The Free Library of Philadelphia

1

Library as Stoa

Great library buildings have always been aspirational. They are places designed to serve a complex set of social and cultural needs and they are faced with the challenge of integrating the inspirational with the functional.

In a world of pervasive digital information, the association of the library with print culture and the physical book obscures its embeddedness in the social processes of knowledge production and cultural creation. As institutions, libraries have always been overdetermined, sustaining within their confines a range of activities from reading and research to lectures and musical events, connecting people and ideas, providing access to new technologies, facilitating various literacies, serving as gathering spaces and places of respite, preserving the social and cultural record, opening up pathways to self-education and continuous learning, and enhancing their host community's sense of cohesion and civic connection. While libraries will continue to serve as repositories of stuff, they nowadays are focused more than ever on social and intellectual engagement as much as they are on material collections.

Because they embrace such a various set of functions, their architectural precedents are defined by a range of contexts—many of them connected to ideals of public space. In classical Greek architecture, a *stoa* is a public walkway along a colonnade, typically along the perimeter of a building complex: a common space where people stroll and converse. Craig Dykers of Snøhetta has likened walking along a *stoa* to walking through a grove of trees, with its alternating areas of light and shade and its capacity to induce a meditative state. In email correspondence to a number of us working on the project during the design of the Charles Library, Craig shared some reflections on the deep historical valence of this perception. Writing about Academus, the mythical savior of the city of Athens, Craig said:

> *Academus was ... buried in an area of northwestern Athens in a place*
> *seen as important to Athena, the goddess of wisdom, who sheltered*
> *it as a sanctuary. This would seem to be an auspicious place to*
> *bury Academus since his wisdom was widely acknowledged by the*
> *Athenians after saving the city from the battle with the Trojans.*

At Academus' burial place there apparently existed [a] grove of trees. I am not sure if this was by design or if they had naturally occurred there, but these trees were linked to the sacred grove planted at Academus' birthplace near Cephissus. This grove in Athens was given the name "the Grove of the Academe," a name that would later become Plato's Academy, or the Akademia. This lineage becomes the root of the word academia, used similarly today to connote a place of wisdom.

These groves of trees create for me the first step of better understanding a library. The trees are divine, they represent gathering and wisdom that arose from conflict. They are a natural element meant to inspire.[1]

Here, then, this social space of the *stoa* is identified as a space of inspiration at the heart of the academy. This was an anchoring principle in our conversations about the possibilities for the Charles Library at Temple. But that high concept has a counterweight in the continuing requirement for practical impacts: for quiet and/or active study spaces, for collaborative work environments, for learning and research support, for access to the new technologies of scholarship, and for the continuing storage and use of physical materials. Writing in *The Library Beyond the Book*, Jeffrey Schnapp and Matthew Battles make note of the foundational intertwining of these inward and outward faces:

…libraries have always been institutions built upon a paradox. On the one hand, they are places of enclosure: fortified bastions, sites of burial and storage of treasures; places of retreat from the din of the market place; sacred precincts and temples devoted to contemplation and prayer; self-sufficient worlds where … lovers of the word, hold court. On the other hand, libraries open up onto the world: the noise of the street invades their sacred precinct; their collections cannot be built up without connections between capital and periphery …; connections between societies at large and communities of learning.[2]

---

1. Personal email, November 6, 2014.
2. Harvard University Press, 2014, p. 27. My quotation here contains several ellipses indicating deletion of some phrases from the Schnapp and Battles text that reference the historical context of classical era libraries but the connection to continuing and library characteristics is explicit throughout the argument.

Schnapp and Battles liken the large-scale collections storage mission of libraries to a kind of entombment and preservation, linking it to social memory but also to a set of sacred practices, creating a place where the dead voices live on. I am reminded by this, of the massive vault that forms the northwest quadrant of the Charles Library and that holds the high-density automated storage and retrieval system where the great bulk of our collections are stored. While in one respect you can view that impressive instance of early twenty-first century robotic technology as somewhat mausoleum-like, it was engineered to keep those entombed voices accessible and actively engaged with ongoing learning and research.

But there's more to it. Let me again turn to Schnapp and Battles:

> *The library is both a cemetery and the livebrary: a place of intensified, deeper sociality and communion, a place of burial and mummification that equals a place of constant renewal, reactivation and conversation across the centuries. As the storage/entombment function of "the book" (as once understood) sets over the horizon, these activation functions again move to the fore: what are we going to do with all that space that was devoted to storage in the form of stacks? What forms of conversation do we require or desire? The democratization of this once-enclosed world … [has] given rise to a vastly enriched world of knowledge forms, and defined a new set of civic and public functions for temples of learning.* [3]

The Charles Library is one attempt to instantiate a response to Schnapp and Battles' provocations, in the context both of Temple University's urban public nature and its evolving institutional identity and of the historical environment and dynamic present day reality of the city of Philadelphia.

As you will read in the essays that follow, the planning and design of the Charles Library was richly informed by study of the Temple campus as a built environment—and that

---

3. Ibid., p. 29.

Library as Stoa

environment itself was viewed as an ever evolving embodiment of the University's mission, character, and ambitions. Equally important, planning and design looked not only inward at the campus but also outward at the city and especially at the University's surrounding North Philadelphia neighborhood and the uses that the neighborhood's residents make of the campus and of the University's library facilities. Creating a library building that would serve the University in many practical ways but that would also welcome in the broader community as a beacon and attractor was central to our early conversations.

Those conversations were wide-ranging and imaginative and some of the illustrations of that early work in this book convey the energy the collaborators in this project—the Snøhetta design team and Temple University staff—brought to their engagements. We identified and discussed many metaphors for a contemporary research library and its functions and attempted to align those metaphors with key elements of the Temple context. We spoke of gateways, crossroads, courtyards, studios, and forums; the library as an entry point to the world of learning and knowledge; the library as a place of shelter and space for reflection, for our students and faculty as for our community neighbors.

Elements of those conversations found their way into the building's final design—in the large cantilevered arch that calls you into the library from Thirteenth Street and that implicitly forms a forum or courtyard that will face the green space that will front the library on its east side; in the spiraling wood-clad atrium that expresses an organic warmth and beckons from the exterior; and in the open, flexible, and technologically-capacious work and study areas that support learning, scholarly pursuit, and creative endeavor. Figuratively in the context of a university, a library can be, above all else, a crossroads, a place where the various disciplines meet and intersect, where the community's scope and diversity become visible, where unexpected intellectual and cultural collisions stimulate fresh thinking. The Charles Library sits at a literal crossroads, at the intersection of Polett and Liacouras Walks, the two busiest pedestrian thoroughfares on campus, pathways that connect the buildings that house the various schools and colleges at the center of campus. It's a building that expresses a twinned purpose throughout, embracing the noise, dynamism and heterogeneity both of the University and of the contemporary urban environment while also providing a place for reading, study, and quiet reflection. Its glass-enclosed fourth floor contains traditional browsing book stacks, and daylight from that top level cascades down through the central oculus to the bustling public square that is the first floor atrium, expressing a connection between the place of knowledge and the life of the street. These are but a few of the ways the Charles Library realizes some of the touchstone images and metaphors that informed its design.

It has been an extraordinary privilege to be part of the team that shaped this building. The Snøhetta designers brought to the task deep creative vision, a sophisticated understanding of the library as a social and cultural enterprise, and a focused sensitivity to the institutional and urban communities the building will serve. It is my hope that the Charles Library will inspire generations of Temple students and faculty and will energize learning and research at a dynamic public urban university for decades to come.

JOE LUCIA
Dean, Temple Libraries

2

Social and Cultural Memory
The Idea of Library

Human social and cultural history can be traced through four great language-related inflection points. First was language's invention: the advent of symbolic communication. Second was the invention of script writing—a further symbolization. Third, the printing press. We are witnessing the unfolding of the fourth transformative moment, which is the assertive transformation of the intellectual record into a network of flowing digital content. All of these changes were unprecedented. All were transformational. Each advancement liberated knowledge, thought, and cultural expression from their previous limitations. These moments are foundational in our cognitive apparatus and also in our ways of shaping, expressing, and recording what we know and what we do.

The contemporary moment is historically unique in its visibility. The accelerated process of change is observed as it unfolds, and it necessitates the reinvention of the institutional structures tasked with carrying out the core mission of accommodating the change. New processes, new structures, and new approaches must be introduced while still carrying forward the traditional missions of learning and remembering, of accessing research and creating it. And amid these large-scale changes and their deep institutional impacts, the library must function simultaneously as an agent of change and a memory institution.

JOE LUCIA
Dean, Temple Libraries
Architecture and the Evolution of the 21st Century Cultural Memory Institution Symposium, Temple University, February 10, 2015

Library as Aspirational Space

A library houses and stores, collects and displays: a site of memorable experience and a meeting place of people and knowledge. As a design project, the library presents opportunities to fully focus on intentionality and the reflective value of architecture. Throughout history, libraries have been places of learning, dialogue, debate, and discussion; places of knowledge acquisition and creation; places to archive written documents in the form of scrolls or tablets or books; exclusive places associated with colleges and universities, and inclusive community gathering places.

A library's conception and design considers spaces and their uses, but more importantly the design of a library can reflect the aspirations of a culture. In the case of Temple University's Charles Library, the project was an occasion to reflect on the culture of both the University and of the city of Philadelphia; in this physical context, the Charles Library projects and extends into the future and represents ideas of innovation and openness in learning and research.

In terms of architectural ideas, the Charles Library exists in the context of the library as a type, which is derived in a general sense from Enlightenment ideas of architecture. In the middle of the nineteenth century a group of young French architects, including Henri Labrouste, were attracted to the utopian-socialist ideas of Henri de Saint-Simon, which challenged artists to be critical of the status quo and push toward a better future. According to the Saint-Simonians as society progresses it alternates between critical phases—which are dominated by individual competition—and organic phases—which are cooperative and dedicated to a common goal.[1] It was believed that each of these great phases could be associated with a single building type that served as the focus of that society's greatest aspirations. This was considered to be the temple in the ancient world, the cathedral in

1. See Frank Manuel, *The New World of Henri de Saint-Simon* (Cambridge: Harvard University Press, 1956) for an analysis of this theory of progress.

1

2

the Middle Ages, and, for Labrouste, it would be the library that would embody the spirit of the modern age. As such, he designed the Bibliothèque Saint-Geneviève (1838-50) as a monument to books—synthesizing new techniques in iron construction, gas lighting, ventilation, and heating into a design that welcomed students from around Paris's Latin Quarter into the luminous reading room on the top floor. (FIGS. 1-2) The nineteenth century Enlightenment library, both in terms of idea and configuration, has remained with us. But with changes in information delivery and the pace of information production, the architecture of a library as a monument to books, is challenged.

The architectural expression of libraries has taken many forms and the thread of interest from a design standpoint comes from the rewards related to understanding the coexistence and relationship of people and knowledge. The design of a library often reflects a community's high-minded aspirations through the specific articulation of the architectural space and form. Libraries can be powerful and inspiring places that present the vastness of knowledge, where books and space combine to demonstrate the never-ending potential of intellectual productivity. For some, libraries are places for thought and wonder in splendid isolation. A well-designed library consecrates the pursuit of knowledge—offering refuge and a place to encounter civilization's memory to seekers of information and lovers of learning amidst the quiet and the smell of books, in beautiful light, warmth, and comfort.

Distinct types of libraries reflect a spectrum of values and ideas. Academic libraries, because of their mission and aims, differ in architectural expression from community and public lending libraries. Common to all is the need to balance social space against and in relation to book storage. This is a practical consideration, but the spatial implications of the relationship of books and people are also an expression of design intent and emphasis. While a library's primary role can shift, it must always serve several programmatic roles along the spectrum of book-place to people-place: at once a warehouse, a place of community, a place of sacred encounter with texts, a place of production.

At its core, a library is a repository of social and cultural

Social and Cultural Memory: The Idea of Library

3

4

5

memory. How we value and use collections reflects how we appraise social and cultural memory and cultural heritage. Our use of collections over time reflects their impact and relevance. This is particularly significant in the present time when considering how the acquisition of information and the production of knowledge can influence architectural expression. In turn, how a library's architecture asserts its position along the continuum of social space and storage space, as well as how it creates image and deploys space, can determine the impact the institution has as a cultural and intellectual change agent. The nature of the space as a meeting place of person and material will determine how people physically and productively engage with the space.

The University Library

University libraries from the mid-twentieth century—among them Temple University's own Paley Library, opened in 1966—prioritized the function of book storage over providing social space for people to gather and learn. (FIG. 3-5) While university libraries have often been designed to function as warehouses, especially in modern times, where space is prioritized in terms of housing and keeping books, they have also been social centers, where community-based activities are included as part of the information stream. The university library as a type reflects the aspirations of its time, its place, and the broader institution that incorporates it. This is illustrated in the Philadelphia context, on the campus of the University of Pennsylvania, for example, where the Fisher Fine Arts Library and its neighbor, the Van Pelt Library, differ in ways that express the particularities of when they were built and the directions that Penn was taking at the respective times of their conception. (FIGS. 6-7) At Temple University, the new Charles Library is situated adjacent to Paley Library and represents a wholly different idea of library, of Temple, and of both academia and community.[2] Van Pelt and Paley, respectively Penn's and

2. The original portion of the Anne and Jerome Fisher Fine Arts Library (1891) was designed by Frank Furness; the Charles Patterson Van Pelt Library (1962), was designed

6

7

Temple's libraries from the 1960s, are forms of architectural expression in which the buildings manifest the priority given to knowledge and information through the housing of books and collections and assert their importance by their centrality to their campuses. The Charles Library at Temple, like Penn's Fisher Fine Arts Library, also occupies a central position, but these two libraries from different eras are designed to be inspirational in their deployment of space, adjacencies, and building details as much or more so than by the collections and books they house.

American college and university campuses often are memorable because of unified architectural elements, styles, and materials. The continuity of architecture in a campus works in conjunction with overall plans using landscape and pathways as settings.

The interior spaces of buildings, especially for major public buildings on a campus, add to a campus network of open space and structure. On campuses where revival styles are used to unify a campus, the architecture is memorable in part because of the continuity that the architectural style provides. Libraries are often prominently featured buildings in the campus. In the late-nineteenth and early-twentieth centuries numerous architects turned to the Collegiate Gothic style—an architecture that was purposely reminiscent of Oxford and Cambridge Universities—on many campuses across the United States to convey a consciousness of history and a belief in the importance of record and memory. This includes the contributions of Cope and Stewardson to the campuses of Bryn Mawr, the University of Pennsylvania, and Princeton; of Ralph Adams Cram to the campus of Princeton; of Charles Klauder to the campuses of the University of Pittsburgh, Pennsylvania State University, and more. (FIGS. 8-10) The style has produced some of the most memorable university libraries across the country, including the Suzzallo Library at the University of Washington (Bebb and Gould, 1926) and the Sterling Memorial Library at Yale University (James Gamble Rogers, 1930). (FIGS. 11-12)

by Harbeson, Hough, Livingston & Larson; the Samuel L. Paley Library (1966) was designed by Nolen & Swinburne.

8

9

10

11

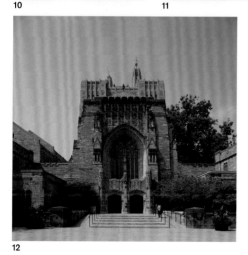

12

The university library is often designed and put forth as a sacred space. Planners and architects have long emphasized the idea of a library as a treasure house of knowledge. Their interiors are places in which individual readers and inquirers can find inspiration and connection with something larger. In a public facing role, the architecture of the university library in the United States can be among the most ecclesiastical in the built environment, maintaining the campus's revival styles with gothic arches and stained glass windows, vaulted spaces and a variety of structurally-articulated interior volumes. In this kind of architecture, the spaces reflect aspirations of research and learning and range from large communal open areas to small, intimate spaces where one can sit comfortably for hours on end. The qualities of light and sound in a library's interior—from brightly lit to shadowed and from quiet to reverberating—enhance the experience, highlighting the architectural features that make the spaces comfortable and the place memorable.

Temple University and the Charles Library

The historical core of Temple University's campus includes several Collegiate Gothic buildings dating from the early part of the twentieth century that align along Broad Street, one of Philadelphia's major thoroughfares. William Harold Lee's

13

124 PROPOSED "TEMPLE OF LEARNING," TEMPLE UNIVERSITY, PHILADELPHIA, PA.

BROAD STREET AND MONTGOMERY AVENUE   2692-29

14

Carnell and Conwell Halls, dating from the mid- to late-1920s, are the southern flank and only completed part of the 350-foot-high Temple of Learning, a building that was planned to accommodate the entire campus. (FIGS. 13-14) When completion of the Temple of Learning was abandoned, new buildings were added. The addition of Mitten Hall, a building for student activities, and Sullivan Memorial Library (now Sullivan Hall) in the 1930s, also designed by Lee, continued north along Broad Street. The new buildings were sited adjacent to the University's initial buildings, the Romanesque Revival Baptist Temple (now Temple Performing Arts Center) and College Hall designed by Thomas P. Lonsdale and dating from the 1890s, to form the architectural identity of the Temple campus. Mitten Hall is separated from Sullivan Hall—two of the campus's most notable buildings—by a wide walkway entrance perpendicular to Broad Street. The walkway is marked by an iron gate along Broad Street, creating a signature landmark on a campus where the majority of architecture is defined by neutrality and campus spaces parallel sidewalks. This section of campus is essentially its northwest corner and has served as its misplaced architectural heart. The iron gate has been one of only a few memorable places on campus, serving as a ceremonial entrance to the University—a literal gateway to the campus and the only access point that provides a sense of arrival or transition from the city to the institution of higher learning within. (FIG. 15)

The historical core of the campus, aligned along Broad Street, was augmented in the 1960s and 1970s and rendered strangely peripheral with a major campus expansion to the east. (FIG. 16) Building within the urban grid this expansion was realized with modernist buildings and campus spaces knit into the urban fabric of North Philadelphia. The cohesive campus expansion plan and many of the buildings included in it were designed by Nolen & Swinburne, including Paley Library, which is located on the south edge of a plaza ringed by other modernist buildings. Along with the plaza and its Bell Tower, Paley served as an important component in creating a center on a campus particularly resistant to such ordering. (FIG. 17)

Social and Cultural Memory: The Idea of Library

15

16

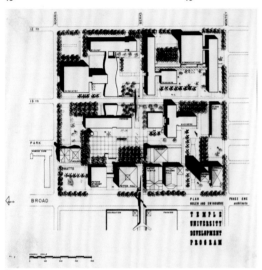

17

18

Paley's interior spaces reflect the campus architectural trends of its day. Tall windows and an exterior gallery space ring its double-height main floor on three sides, while a mezzanine is located along the south wall. The main floor serves as an inviting architectural feature, suffused in natural light. (FIG. 18) Stairs to the lower level land close to a south-facing room, which faces onto a garden. The upper floors are more utilitarian, serving as a warehouse for books that have spaces carved out within the stacks for tables and study carrels. Book storage is the priority; the experience of users, secondary. Offices are mainly internal on the upper and lower floors.

The animating idea of the new Charles Library was to provide the Temple University campus with a unifying center. It was conceived to be a common place for students, faculty, and community to work and engage in research, scholarship, and related academic pursuits. The Library highlights the University's rich array of collections, and prioritizes means of access to services, as well as digital and physical materials. This accessibility is announced by its location on the campus, and its centralized services provide convenience while representing the ideas of centrality and usefulness.

Located along Thirteenth Street on a site bounded by Norris Street to the north, Liacouras Walk to the west, and Polett Walk to the south, the placement of the Charles Library slightly reorients the campus center. The new building sits on the site of a now-demolished modernist building on the Bell Tower Plaza's western edge. The selection of this site makes the library an important element in the campus order and the ample open space around it gives it visibility from any direction. The future five-acre campus quadrangle, planned to the east of the Charles Library, will incorporate the Bell Tower Plaza and shift the campus center northwards in the grid, building on Nolen & Swinburne's initial campus plan (1954), but increased in size to create a place in the grid that builds on the legacy of public urban squares in Philadelphia.[3] (FIG. 19) When completed, the combination of

3. The prominent public urban squares are the four from the 1683 Holme plan for

19

20

library and open space continues the tradition that was presented with Paley Library and the Bell Tower Plaza, of using the library and adjacent open space as a core for the campus and symbol of its identity.

Library Design

The vision for the Charles Library started with a concept of the library as an inspirational center for the campus community that sits comfortably in the urban fabric of Temple University. As an intellectual, social, and cultural center, the library was conceived as a place to cultivate and support dynamic engagement, bringing together people with information, tools, and services.[4] Snøhetta was brought on board to help realize this vision, serving as the lead design architect and landscape architect for the project. The Snøhetta project team was shortlisted for the project after an international search in 2012. Snøhetta's collaborative approach to design—favoring the social environment of architecture—was a good fit for the Temple library project. This was well demonstrated in their built works. And their careful consideration of the role a library can play in building community was apparent, beginning with the Alexandria Library and also including the then-recent Hunt Library at North Carolina State University. Design for the Temple library began with a workshop and charrette that included representatives from Snøhetta, Stantec (the executive architect), and Temple University.[5] (FIG. 20) Using the baseline program developed by brightspot strategy, the workshop and charrette generated a number of different schemes that addressed the tight site and adjacencies, ideas of movement on the campus at the prime location of the library, and the internal relationships of services. Five distinct early schemes emerged from this initial exercise that

Philadelphia, commissioned by William Penn, now incorporated into the central urban fabric: Rittenhouse, Logan, Franklin, and Washington Squares. A fifth, Center Square, is now covered by the Philadelphia City Hall.

4. Snøhetta Stantec, Temple University Library, Schematic Design Report. September 19, 2014, p. 7.

5. Project participants and consultants are included in Project Credits on page 236.

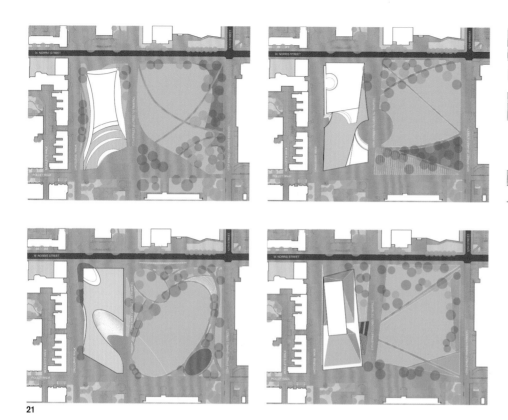

21

each shared the common idea of linking the library with the open quadrangle. (FIG. 21) These provided the bones for the eventual project as the library design developed and incorporated the larger design gestures into two selected schemes that were explored in more detail. Elements of the final entry sequence—the arches, the stairway, and the oculus—were present in both of the selected schemes. On the exterior, the upper terrace and green roof, as well as the importance of the southeast corner of the site were also recognized through this process.

The library's exterior presence is characterized by four distinct elements: the building's solid wall, which presents the building as a mass, wraps the building and is opened or perforated where interior light is needed; the openings—the east-facing arched

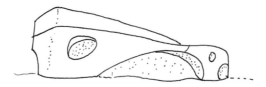

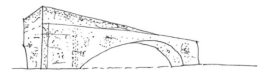

22

Above: Early studies exploring facade texture and materiality.
Right: Concept models generated during early workshops with
Temple, Snøhetta, and Stantec, exploring potential concepts for
massing, program organization, and relationships between the
library and planned open space on campus.

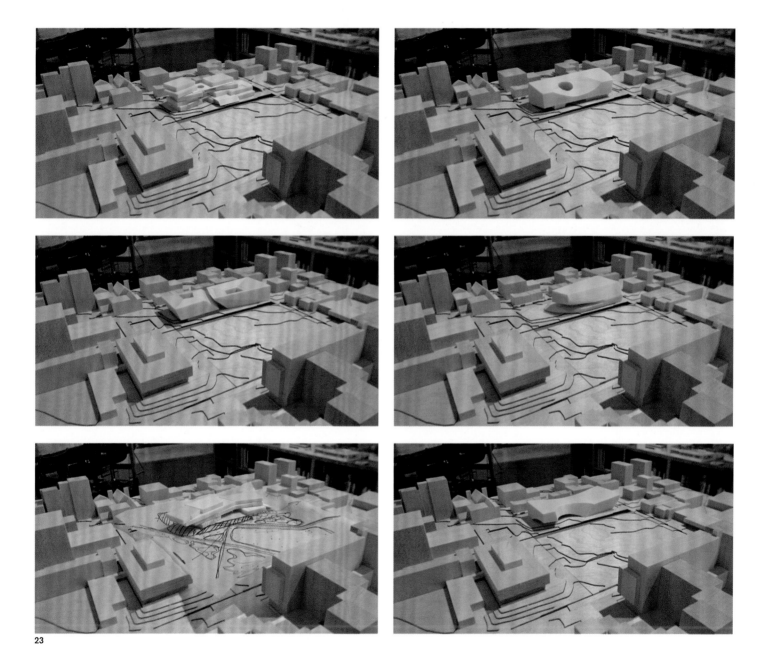

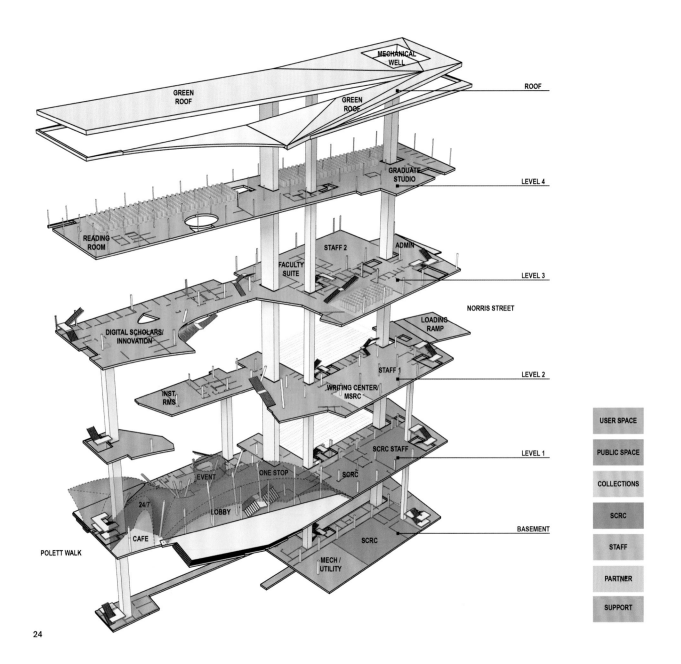

MECHANICAL WELL

GREEN ROOF

GREEN ROOF

ROOF

GRADUATE STUDIO

LEVEL 4

READING ROOM

STAFF 2

ADMIN

FACULTY SUITE

LEVEL 3

NORRIS STREET

DIGITAL SCHOLARS/ INNOVATION

LOADING RAMP

STAFF 1

LEVEL 2

INST. RMS

WRITING CENTER/ MSRC

SCRC STAFF

LEVEL 1

SCRC

EVENT

ONE STOP

24/7

LOBBY

SCRC

BASEMENT

POLETT WALK

CAFE

SCRC

MECH / UTILITY

USER SPACE

PUBLIC SPACE

COLLECTIONS

SCRC

STAFF

PARTNER

SUPPORT

24

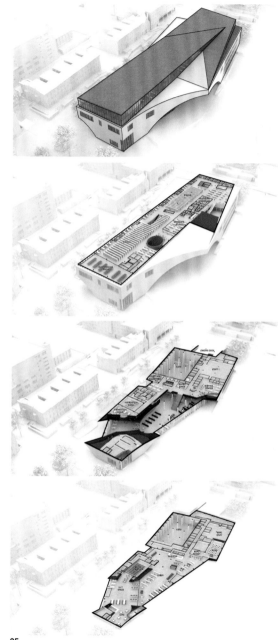

Design Development
Left: Exploded plan view of Charles Library.
Right: Axonometric floor plans of Charles Library

25

26

27

28

opening that gives a gesture of welcome and connects through the interior to the mid-façade opening to the west, and to the corner arch at the southwest corner; the glass-box reading room that caps the building and is held within the mass to the south and extends beyond it to the north; and finally, the green roof, an inclined plane that serves as a gestural element of extension. (FIG. 26)

The library provides an inspirational experience and serves as a memorable work of architecture. Understanding it as such a spatial environment allows one to envision its survival long past its initial use and intended function. Before deciding how to house books and accommodate people, or how to bring users face-to-face with the artifacts of social and cultural memory, an architect must first undertake to design a space in which people will want to be. As such, the Charles Library joins other inspirational campus buildings as a piece of architecture that will withstand the test of time. These kinds of campus buildings can be or have been adapted to new and unanticipated uses because they are welcoming, interesting, engaging environments, and those qualities supersede the spaces' initial prescribed purposes.

The Charles Library design responds to the current needs of Temple University but is flexible enough to allow for the inevitable shifts in the needs of both the library and the University in the short term and over the lifespan of the building. Circulation and spatial adjacencies within the Charles Library are well considered and designed so that the library patron understands the discreet and specific functions. A primary aim of the architecture is to welcome people, to invite them to enter, to stay, and to do things. From each entrance the library presents itself as a whole through the integration of several architectural elements, including the entrance arches, the central staircase, and the oculus that admits light from the fourth-floor reading room down into the main lobby on the ground floor. (FIG. 27) The library's primary entrances invite people in from several major pedestrian intersections and campus spaces. (FIGS. 28–29) They are on the southeast and west, with an entrance into a 24-7 area of the library also open from the southwest corner. From any direction, a person enters under a portion of the wood-clad arches. With the entrances defined

Social and Cultural Memory: The Idea of Library

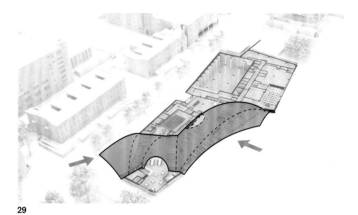

29

30

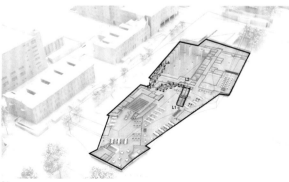

31

by these elements, the view into the library is guided up by the staircase through the center of the building. Light enters the glass box at the top of the building, a reading room that contains book stacks and tables for study. Spatially and organizationally, this light passes through the oculus and illuminates the atrium at the lower level. The fourth floor offers books, out in the open and ready at hand, confirming the essential idea of a library. The selection is weighted in favor of books that are commonly handled, including materials in architecture, the visual arts and art history, as well as the performing arts, specifically music. With all of the Charles Library books on site and quickly accessed from the Automated Storage and Retrieval System (ASRS) or available in digital format, the fourth floor collection is complementary to the collection as a whole, providing access to print material in areas of research where the central role of the book is not easily replaced.

From all locations within the library the wood-clad arches and oculus are visible to the library user, serving as a visual orientation device. Open and spacious, it provides spaces to gather, read, and research in a welcoming and well-lit environment. Each level has a sitting area that provides visual communication to the floors above and below as well as to the campus outside. The visual path connects the various illuminated spaces that surround the central arch and oculus as the user climbs to the traditional, recognizable fourth-floor reading room. The major architectural features are joined on the third and fourth floor by another major feature, the green roof, which directs the gaze upward along an inclined plane that parallels Thirteenth Street.

The library is designed so people will utilize the stairs as their primary means of moving through the building. (FIGS. 30–31) The location, openness, and connectivity provided by stairs make them a fun and interesting place to both see and be seen by others, rendering them as an important social space within the building. By design, the stairs encourage a commitment to physicality and in doing so conscript the body to the requirements of the architecture. The body is engaged, one's heart rate is elevated and breathing deepens. The body is also guided up or down the

32

stairs as a social space, which serves in part as a form of protection for the quieter areas and spaces of concentration that are found deeper in spaces screened off and secreted away from the central space. The architecture welcomes and guides, leads the user to spaces, and protects some spaces from noise and activity. The users can orient themselves and make choices, empowered and grounded by the experience of the architecture.

The range of public spaces in the library, combining aspirational qualities with functional aims, is designed to be flexible enough to accommodate current uses and purposes not yet anticipated. To achieve this, the interior of the library uses transparency and layering of space that connects the parts of the building; this can be exhibited in the scale of spaces and adjacencies. For example, book storage is compacted into the ASRS in the northwest portion of the building, and the space freed up by this high-density storage is used for social space, maker space, seating, and services. Further, it affords a position of greater prominence to Temple's collections, and an accessibility they've never before been afforded. These collections—which are meant to be seen, shared, and used—link the University and its collections to the city.

The location for retrieving books from storage is visible from the main library space but in an area that is partially enclosed and quiet. Library Special Collections occupies the first floor in the northeast quadrant of the building, directly adjacent to the access point for special collections storage. Special Collections is functionally convenient yet prominently situated so that it can serve a primary role in the campus and be easy to access for patrons from outside the University community. Open shelves are located on the fourth floor to the north of the main space, and there are a variety of individual and group workspaces, classrooms, and seminar spaces distributed across the third and fourth floors. Other featured spaces—the event space on the first floor, partner spaces for academic assistance, the scholars studio, digital scholar and maker spaces, and immersive visualization and gaming spaces—are prominent and visible to any library patron, and their incorporation within the library's main space bestows on them a context within research and scholarship, such that they are recognized as tools of and conduits for learning. This scholarly contextualization is strengthened through the visibility that many of these spaces have from the exterior of the library, which situates them within the academic campus in general, while their interior orientation back to the oculus and stairway in the center connect them to the library in particular. (FIG. 32)

The Charles Library is an environment that encourages learning and offers a variety of support services. Its technology environment is mobile and fluid; its services exist in spaces for public gathering and events as well as one-on-one and small group conversations. The Charles Library complements other services on the Temple campus where more traditional uses of information technology already exist. The library houses around fifty small- and medium-sized rooms equipped with a variety of tools for people to work together in groups small and large and supports and makes available a variety of digital devices within a dense, pervasive wireless environment. As is expected in the research library environment, it is conceived as a place for learning along a wide range of modalities from personal interaction and perusing books to engaging with digital technologies at various scales. Digital tools are adjacent to physical materials, collection areas, and books, providing an environment that encourages work across platforms and with unique materials. Librarians and other teaching and learning specialists in the building provide support for learning and inquiry.

Library Collections in the Digital Age

In the digital age there is a prescient question to be asked about how physical collections maintain their relevance long into the future. The answer lies in the question itself: a digital future *assures* the relevance of the physical collection. The materiality of these archives will remain absolutely crucial, but their digital avatars are their best possible advertisement. It allows for collaboration across the city and the world in ways that were never possible before. Where the Special Collections were housed in

33

the basement of Paley Library, their presence as a memorable destination with a prominent location in the Charles Library assures their relevance in the city. (FIG. 33)

Temple Libraries Special Collections reflect the University's strength and contribution to the city as a keeper of cultural memory. As a collecting organization Temple is renowned for its broad and deep set of archival materials related to the social, cultural, and intellectual life of Philadelphia. This is particularly true of the Urban Archives, whose collection reflects the everyday rhythm of the city. It was established in 1967 and its holdings extend from the nineteenth to the twenty-first century, providing rich documentation of the details of everyday life—experienced in context—of the groups that provide the texture and the unique historical dimensions of a particular urban region, including ethnic organizations, social clubs, nonprofit enterprises, and arts organizations. Most collecting organizations in the 1960s took an interest in the works of great academics and world-renowned experts, or in the papers of projects they themselves had sponsored. The Urban Archives re-imagined the function of collections and the nature of social history holdings. They include the records of local businesses, like the Pennsylvania Railroad Company, and community organizations and nonprofits. Comprised of millions of images and clippings from the Philadelphia Evening Bulletin; newsreel footage from KYW and WPVI; and 100 photographic collections from the City Parks Association, the Gray Panthers, and others, the Urban Archives is a sociological lens on the life of the city, but it is also a broad body of documentation that provides specific, particular, and local information, a record of the region's contemporary culture and unassuming history written as it happened. (FIGS. 34-36) These things were not traditionally thought of historically because they weren't yet history.

Building a library in a period of transformation is an interesting proposition. In the digital era, information is more portable and accessible than ever, and the extent of ready access to digital material raises persistent questions about the library as an architectural type: what is the point of making a space for knowledge in the digital era? These questions are borne out of preconceived

34–36

notions of a library, and ignore the crucial function of a library at a time when the sheer amount of digital information is overwhelming. Libraries and archives are places where that deluge can be mediated and made more comprehensible and digestible for the users. The current era presents an opportunity to frame the architecture of a library in different terms, addressing the coincidence of print and digital information and the opportunity for knowledge acquisition alongside knowledge production. With this in mind the team was inspired by Snøhetta's thinking on the typology of the Greek *stoa* as a model for the contemporary library. *Stoas* played a major role in the life of Greek cities, supporting a wide range of interesting uses. They were meeting places, places to display public notices, places for public dining, places for people wanting shelter from the rain or sun, and places to learn from the great philosophers of the age.[6] Socrates could often be found in the Stoa of Zeus Eleutherios, and Zeno of Citium, the founder of the Stoic school of thought that took its name from the building type, met and taught his followers in the Stoa Poikile on the northern edge of the Athenian Agora. Furthermore, the *stoa* functioned as an architectural framing device for the public open space of the agora, tying the two together as the heart of

6. See J.J. Coulton, *The Architectural Development of the Greek Stoa* (Oxford: Clarendon Press, 1976) for more on the variety of uses to be found in the Greek stoa.

the civic life of Greek cities. In early phases of the design process, Snøhetta meditated on the idea of the library as stoa:

> *We appreciate that the library has in many ways come full circle, from its beginnings in the ancient Greek stoa, to the now-dated but still existent model of a large-scale materials repository, and once again towards a more versatile, broadly accommodating space for learning, creating, and sharing of ideas. Combining this notion with the most innovative available technology, the new Library will place Temple among the forefront of progressive universities.*[7]

The current cultural conversation about the library as an environment is less constrained by physical storage and more focused on interaction and engagement. Social space is concerned with the people who occupy it; storage space with the things that are housed in it, and the relationship between the two creates opportunities for discovery and knowledge creation. When there are more social spaces and more activity in a library, the things that are stored have increased impact. Models of future use and future need are based on the social dimensions that are shaped by new tools, technologies, and approaches to information and research resources. Solutions are provisional and experimental. Contribution to the intellectual debate and cultural production is no longer limited to writing a book or publishing an article as the rules shift about who is allowed to join the dialogue. In a university setting the definition of a scholar has expanded with, for example, undergraduate students and members of the public now included in the intellectual debate.

7. Snøhetta Stantec, Temple University Library, Schematic Design Report. September 19, 2014, p. 6.

3

On Site
Construction
Documentation

On Site: Construction Documentation

On Site: Construction Documentation

On Site: Construction Documentation

On Site: Construction Documentation

On Site: Construction Documentation

On Site: Construction Documentation

On Site: Construction Documentation

On Site: Construction Documentation

4

Community and Cultural Identity
Stories, Spaces, Functions

Community input as a starting point in the design of a library is of primary importance, but asking people about what they want in a library will yield answers based on a pre-existing idea of a library. Ask people about their activities and to describe the services they need and they can be very clear—not only about what their needs are and how they're changing, but also about precisely what would meet those needs.

This is the fundamental tension in project planning. When we ask people about needs, in smaller conversations we hear lots of new things, but then on surveys we hear about the typical concerns in a library: "We need more books"; "We need more quiet space" because people can often only imagine a slightly improved version of today as opposed to something totally new. New ideas about space use must balance with understanding traditional needs, and a productive process allows for new uses while recognizing the integrity of what still works.

ELLIOT FELIX
brightspot strategy, April 4, 2017,
Stories, Spaces, Functions Symposium, Temple University

Community and Cultural Identity: Stories, Spaces, Functions

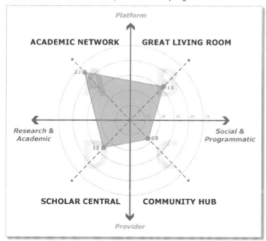

LIBRARY PURPOSE

Research & Academic   *Social & Programmatic*

LIBRARY ROLE

Platform

Academic Network

A global network that offers the tools, infrastructure, and spaces to physically and digitally connect with scholars at Temple and beyond, showcase and exchange ideas, and work in an inspiring atmosphere.

Great Living Room

A magnetic, lively gathering place that offers a variety of spaces to convene, chat, collaborate, and create as well as retreat to concentrate, all supported by a curated selection of resources, services, and tools.

Scholar Central

An extensive system of resources and services in a stimulating and scholarly environment that offers personalized support for finding, retrieving, and using information, along with expert academic feedback and mentorship.

Community Hub

A hub for connecting Temple and the city that offers an extensive catalog of courses, events, and exhibitions. With something for everyone and welcoming public spaces, it's the destination for social learning.

Provider

The future direction of the library is a hybrid of the four scenarios, with a strong pull towards the Academic Network, in which the library is a platform for scholars to digitally and physically connect on a global scale. It will be 2/3 platform and 1/3 provider, and 2/3 research and academics-focused and 1/3 social and programmatic.

1

Stories

An academic research library supports many constituent groups and houses disparate functions, so the early stages of any viable programming process must take into account the needs of students, faculty, staff, and local community; the varied kinds of experiences they're having today; and the uses of a building designed for the acquisition and creation of knowledge.

In the early planning stages for the Charles Library, representatives from brightspot strategy, which specializes in higher education strategic planning and programming, gathered information about the Temple University community's needs and the behavior of its library users. Working with the Snøhetta design team and Temple Library's leadership, brightspot began the process by seeking out stories of user engagement in the University library to aid the process of idea generation. They consulted students, faculty, representatives from the surrounding neighborhood, librarians, maintenance staff, administration, and other stakeholders. These varied groups, the disparate ways they interacted with the university, and the things they would want and use in a library provided a wide array of hopes and ideas. Participants were asked to think about how they learn and how they work; to think about the tools they needed to create and to be productive; and to imagine the future of the library (FIG. 1). These questions, asked in small groups, served two purposes. The questions allowed brightspot to gather information about what a library should be, while also identifying and observing a cross section of the library's community and introducing it to itself. In this latter instance, the process was the beginning of building a community in support of the new library.

Story creation was brightspot's primary method for community engagement, which drove the development of the design program. In programming, brightspot sought answers that would lead to innovative uses of space and deployment of services rather than rote answers of what participants thought a library should be. The narratives were a fundamental guide to the questions and

2

3

discussions that followed and as those narratives were folded into the discussions, workshop participants were asked to then engage with the library not as themselves, but as characters in a story. They were asked to consider the needs of all different types of library users, now and in the future: if a library was a place to learn, to research, to engage, and to create, what would help the users get the most from it?

Story creation provided participants with a shortcut to thinking about library design beyond their own needs and reactions—that quiet library space, those endless books ready to hand—to a consideration of future uses. Their ideas led to new possibilities in space configuration and groupings of previously separate functions, combinations that provided greater flexibility or accommodated a greater range of activities in a space. Three weeks of workshops were carried out using archetypal users—called "personas"—based on behavior, needs, and motivations. The personas provided a helpful view when considering how they might use space, and how they would interact with information and with each other. They aided in envisioning a day in the life of the library, as determined through its users. brightspot created a series of scenarios and goals for each of the archetypal users, involving personal characteristics that might shape what kind of experiences they would seek out in the library. The process helped shape the unique circumstances created by specifics of the site, community, and its cultural aspirations. As the design process moved forward and the architecture evolved, the attention paid to attributes as disparate as human needs, the site, and the culture of a community helped guide the project towards a fitting conclusion that avoided prescriptive solutions.

With design goals related to the role of the research library, its function, and its place within the University, some of the central questions for this project revolve around individuals and their use of the library as a new destination on the campus. For example, the Go-Getter persona, coming to the library to do research on a Saturday afternoon, has a couple of hours of time. She needs to be able to find what she's looking for quickly. Another user, say, the Climber, visits to research a Master's program he might be

Community and Cultural Identity: Stories, Spaces, Functions

4

5

6

Community and Cultural Identity: Stories, Spaces, Functions

7

8

9

10

11

interested in. Their needs inform their use and learning how to facilitate the most efficient and effective expenditure of time—hers limited, his sporadic—provides critical particulars that serve to shape the allocation of space and resources, thus guiding the foundation of a specific design approach. By considering what the users would do, what their needs and tasks were, brightspot followed each user through a specific scenario: getting help writing a paper, finding research sources, creating a video, and so on. Services to provide the necessary assistance to these personas are both familiar in the historical context and representative of current and future digital-age trends. (FIGS. 12–13)

The programming process, which served as the basis for strategic planning and design, would determine the services that would come to be offered in the library. Temple Libraries had for some time been considering what services could be brought to the new library and what resources those services would require. Certain key spaces and services had first been prototyped and tested in the Paley Library, to anticipate impact, best use, and best practice in the new library. Testing the Innovation Lab and the Digital Scholars Studio at Paley, for instance, provided useful guidance when considering how to implement them in a new space. Even though the prototype could not determine specifically how those services would operate in the Charles Library, it still aided in conceptualizing the shapes, qualities, and adjacencies of spaces there. And there was room for optimism. The Paley Library integration of services was recognized as a major positive development. Charles Library's configuration would allow for greater flexibility and integrative possibilities, and the programmatic elasticity of use and room for innovation promises real help for library users of all types.

The personas were representations of a range of library patrons, but the design process also took into account additional roles when considering the range of uses in the library. One group of users in particular, librarians, highlights the experience of a provider of services. Technological changes drive cultural changes, thereby influencing how knowledge is rendered, recorded, shared, and distributed. As the nature and the requirements of scholarship and research change, the scope of services and role of the librarian shift and expand as well.

To better serve the university community, Temple Libraries has shifted some of its key services in recent years. The addition of roving librarians, for example, has had a positive impact on information literacy. Librarians work with their subject-matter constituents attending class sessions for key courses and introducing discipline-specific research tools to students. They also make themselves available in public spaces outside of the library to increase student accessibility and engagement. In libraries where professional requirements are changing, librarians have new roles to fill, and these new roles require new skills. The demands of the public-facing role present new challenges for librarians, requiring skills including networking, engaging with users to investigate and uncover needs, collaboration, and the promotion of available library services. In recent years, Temple Libraries have experienced increased demand from constituents in the University, city, and region for special collections, and has responded to the demand with a more acute focus on the role of those collections. The inclusion of digital scholarship and a Digital Scholarship Center, first in Paley, then in the Charles Library, provides support for emerging academic programs and scholarly research in new areas of specialization such as the digital humanities and cultural analytics. The provision of these kinds of services in a library setting both reflect and effect changes in the way we think about libraries and how we use them. These shifts represent a move from the library as a place solely to obtain things to a place that also fosters active production—the *making* of things. Further, these changes widen the scope of what is generally accepted as scholarship, which, in turn, is impacting the broader culture of the University campus. In the Charles Library their significance finds expression spatially.

an ideal visit with The Starter

As a transfer student who's trying to brush up her academic skills and stay ahead of her coursework, the Starter is apprehensive about her first semester at Temple and wants thing to go right. She seeks help wherever it's offered and prefers to meet one-on-one so that she can ask questions and get personalized help.

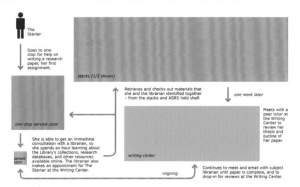

an ideal visit with The Herder

The Herder camps out in the Library as much as possible in order to concentrate and get work done. She often meets with groups and friends in the Library café, her "home base." With the different types of spaces and technology in the Library, she has never had to go elsewhere to work.

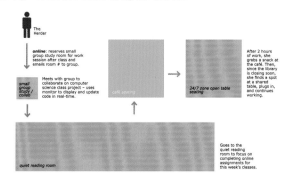

an ideal visit with The Deep Diver

An anthropology PhD candidate, the Deep Diver has established strong ties with the librarians and uses the Library's physical and Special Collections extensively. He often works in the Library and is thrilled to have a space just for graduate students where he can study, store his materials, and meet and converse with graduate students in other disciplines.

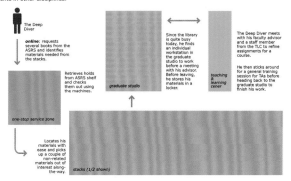

an ideal visit with The Pedagogue

The Pedagogue has assigned his class to conduct a research project on how sharks are portrayed in various fields, e.g.: popular media, biology, sociology, fine arts. Each project team must create a web site to present their research findings and include at least one graphic or video element.

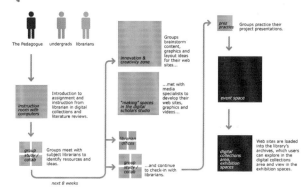

12

13

Equip / Device Storage

Holding Area
Reserves, ILL, E-Z Borrow

Partner Services

Tech. / Collections Processing

Media, Reference Collections

Digital Scholar Studio, Faculty Support Center

Self-Serve ASRS Reserve

Special Collections Research Center

Service Zone

Self-Checkout

Consultation Room

Drop-In Staff Workstations

Service Stations

Triage Station

14

The Role of the Librarian and the Social Ecology of a Library

In addition to the attention given to library users' needs, the programming and early design phases shaped the library's inner social ecology, an environment partially defined by the incorporation of a wide range of resources and services previously dispersed across the campus.[1] As on most college campuses, students at Temple are offered a range of support to be effective in their studies and to master the academic skill set for their programs. The spatial consolidation of these resources and services in the Charles Library incorporated non-librarian academic professionals working there. Situating all these services in one place gives them greater visibility and accessibility, putting critical dimensions of support in a unified environment and placing them directly in the path of students as they enter. (FIG. 14) The services for students are strategic and represent the range of academic assistance a student may require: a tutor, writing support, research assistance from a librarian, and other related services. And conceptually, providing these services in the library setting allows the librarian and staff in the centers to work in partnership, providing more than one service at the same time when necessary.

The library remains a place of research and contemplation, but the definition of a university research library is expanding to adapt to the shifts in services. It has become a place of academic support, an information commons where knowledge is made and not simply acquired. Along with these changes in the library, the definition of a librarian is changing, too. A librarian must have technical skill sets for new ways of using technology in the building, and teaching skill sets for the different kinds of classroom and learning spaces that the new building creates. A librarian has to know what demands special collections will make on the facilities to help curatorial and instructional staff more fully engage classes and help visiting researchers with the unique materials that can inform their research and their inquiries.

---

1. These resources and services include those provided by non-library academic partners such as The Center for Student Success and a range of digital services.

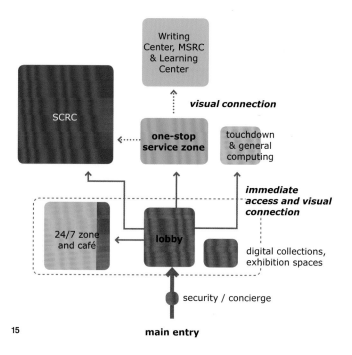

Writing Center, MSRC & Learning Center

SCRC

visual connection

one-stop service zone

touchdown & general computing

immediate access and visual connection

24/7 zone and café

lobby

digital collections, exhibition spaces

security / concierge

main entry

Library professionals already offer a great range of expertise and knowledge. They know the collections in the library and the range of resources. The new library requires an even wider range of expertise and an ability to operate in partnership with other content area experts. Librarians at Charles Library have a triage and coordination function working among non-librarians. They are tasked with keeping a common vision of what students need and what interventions best deal with a student problem, with guiding patrons to the information or the services they seek, and in cases where users don't know what services would best help, librarians can offer guidance about tools, platforms, and other resources. Building inter-professional dialogue between librarians and academic support professionals is paramount to the functioning of the library. In the Charles Library, coordination often begins at the help desk, situated centrally in the library to provide a clear destination for anyone looking for help. **(FIG. 15)**

The rhythm of the librarian's job has changed. It's now much more cyclical and project based. It requires collaboration and flexibility. Where the rhythm of the job used to map to the physical lifecycle of a book, now a librarian works with a class or an individual on the range of resources in all media that are available on a particular topic. The librarian still has to select, buy, catalog, and aid in the search for the right book. And a book must still be cared for through its lifecycle; damage has to be repaired. The ascendancy of digital information and its emerging demands on librarians' time do not obviate these traditional functions, nor do the multiple services offered in the library mean that books no longer need tending to: the lifecycle of the book is simply one of several drivers of the library's mission.

In an age when discovery is as easy as entering a few vague search terms into a web browser, the library is one of many places to go to find information, but it remains a repository of cultural knowledge, and a place to separate useful versus irrelevant information. The management of information has become much more important, and the librarian is the resource to help users find good data, use the right tools, develop the appropriate skills, and avail themselves of the right resources to build and shape a visualization of the data. A librarian offers expertise, and the library of the present and the foreseeable future is a place to craft good new data sets for research, as well as a place where those data are stored for future use.

Function and Placemaking

Charles Library's location, adjacent to the Bell Tower Plaza, was selected to provide continuity to the campus center and to connect the new library with the existing spatial order of the campus. The new library also centralizes the University's collections and books. The limited storage in Paley Library necessitated off-site storage for a majority of its books. Storage of the books in the Charles Library is completely on site and easily accessed through the Automated Storage and Retrieval System (ASRS), which translates to more places for the Temple community to research. Charles' square footage is comparable to Paley's, but with the shift in space usage, Charles has twice the seating capacity with room for around two thousand users. The traditional functions of the library continue, but here they are configured differently with an aim toward greater efficiency, and in service to, for now and into the predictable future, an environment conducive to knowledge-production.

If the two million volumes that make up the library's collection were stored in browsing stacks, the building would have required an additional 125,000 square feet, an unjustifiable amount on a dense urban campus. During the design phase, the University had conversations about how many books a library requires, and there was discussion of a building with no books at all, or a tiny representation thereof. Between the zero-book library and the prospect of a huge building with books stored in stacks, a compromise was reached. The fourth floor would hold approximately two hundred thousand volumes—roughly 10 percent of the total books in the building—in stacks.

Initial design decisions that were made for the Charles Library were intended to exploit opportunities to emphasize and

Community and Cultural Identity: Stories, Spaces, Functions

16

accommodate the urban nature of the Temple campus while also encouraging and promoting the first steps of a new and transformational approach in campus areas ripe for development. The Main Campus of Temple University is a tightly-packed grid, with very few open areas that serve as memorable common spaces. The Snøhetta design team recognized the potential and possibilities that would determine the character of the library site—the large number of students who traverse Liacouras and Polett Walks on any day that classes are in session, the opportunities that arose by creating a corner at the intersection of these important pedestrian ways, the relationship of the Charles Library to the Bell Tower Plaza, and the potential for affecting east-west pedestrian traffic in the area. The design includes features that support and encourage campus pedestrian traffic, including an emphasis on the library's corner of the intersection and an entry located on Liacouras Walk, which aligns with a break in the adjacent rowhouses leading to the Mitten Annex side entry. (FIG. 16) This alignment presented an opportunity to upgrade the Annex entry and to create a more direct connection between these two major public buildings on the campus, a project that will begin in the near future. The campus-altering impact of the new architecture is clear at a glance. As the functions of the Charles Library by nature affect the spatial arrangement of the building's interiors, the building itself, serves as an organizing force for the campus. Located centrally, its use and presence are driving campus transformation.

Placemaking is most associated with planning public spaces, but the concept can also be applied to the creation of a work of architecture. The well-programmed functions of a building serve a utilitarian purpose, and well-designed spaces are appealing, inviting, or inspiring, irrespective of use. But it is the harmonic alignment of programmatic function and architectural character that leads to memorable user experiences of a place. For most library patrons a memorable library is full of places to "be in" in the library, discoverable places among the bookshelves. The intrinsic relationship of book storage and book-use allows for successful placemaking.

17

18

The number of books a research library needs to make it worth the space it takes up has increased substantially over the last century. The growth of source material made the storage of books the primary concern in many university research libraries, a need expressed, for example, in the Paley Library design. The emphasis was placed on the efficient organization of bookshelves and books, while the library user's experience in the space was of secondary concern. In this model, book storage was divorced from the formation of intimate places for study and research; the research library of Paley's era had places for people, but by design those places were distinct from where the books were housed. Any interface between the two was by and large interstitial, user-created, and serendipitous. (FIG. 17) The design of this generation of libraries was concerned with book storage separate from study space. Current trends in library design arise in part from the re-emergence of an important idea: that the making of places within a building can again be a primary attribute of design. The storage of books requires space, and with the number of volumes in a university research library, including Paley, this is most often solved with off-site storage. In this model, the majority of volumes are warehoused elsewhere and retrievable within a few days' time, while the most frequently circulated books remain on site.

The Charles Library presents an interesting case. Keeping all books on-site became a priority during the design phase, but a 300,000-square-foot academic building in an urban context made almost solely for the storage of books would simply cost too much. The model for the Charles Library dedicates a smaller portion of the building to warehousing, and all library resources fit in a much smaller footprint. The ASRS book-storage system makes it possible to house two million volumes in about 25,000 square feet. (FIG. 18)

A comparison of Temple's old and new libraries clearly illustrates the shift in priorities of a university research library. The main entrance to the building now called Paley Hall remains under a portico on the north side of the building and leads into a primary space. In the Charles Library, transparent openings

19

	Current Paley Library		New Library		New Library with All Program Enhancements	
	nsf	%	nsf	%	nsf	%
Public Space	2,950	2%	6,975	5%	12,475	8%
User Space	28,625	20%	52,385	40%	57,675	39%
Collections	69,825	49%	31,013	23%	31,025	21%
Special Collections**	19,375	14%	10,045	8%	9,750	7%
Staff Space	20,225	14%	20,410	15%	23,575	16%
Partner / Complementary	-	0%	8,070	6%	9,925	7%
Building Support	1,900	1%	3,700	3%	3,700	2%
NSF	142,900		132,598		148,125	
GSF	200,000		203,997		227,875	
Net to Gross %	0.71		0.65		0.65	
# user seats (@ avg. 30 sf / seat)^	1,030		2,044		2,340	
% student pop. seated*	3.5%		6.8%		7.8%	

^ 1268 seats @ 24 sf / seat
*assuming 30,000 student FTE (26,000 undergraduate + 4,000 graduate); **SCRC staff space is accounted for in Staff Space

20

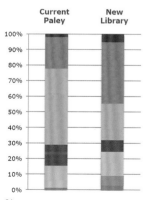

Current Paley   New Library

Space program summary, New Library

Space Type	Net SF
Public	6,975
User	52,125
Collections	31,025
Special Collections	9,450
Staff	21,100
Partners/Complementary	8,175
Building Support	3,700
Total Net SF	**132,550**
Total Gross SF	**203,900**

21

allow a view, even from the outside, through the space and to the east, west and southwest entries. The southwest corner provides access at the intersection of Liacouras and Polett Walks and is dedicated to study space that is accessible for students twenty-four hours a day, seven days a week. (FIG. 19) In Paley, approximately 26 percent of the space was dedicated to open study, while in Charles it will constitute approximately 60 percent of the space. In regards to collections and storage in the libraries these percentages are reversed: approximately 60 percent of the space in Paley served that function while only 25 percent of Charles is dedicated to book storage. Space for library staff, services and building support remains approximately the same in each model, with the addition of expanded academic learning support partner services in Charles. (FIGS. 20–21)

Books are still out and available for browsing in the stacks on the fourth floor adjacent to open study spaces. All of the library's two million volumes are easily accessible; the books in the high-density robotic storage area can be called up and placed in the user's hands in minutes. This lessens the pressure for book storage as a primary role in the library spaces, and the configuration of spaces—both in the browseable stacks and other study areas—is focused on people. The conceptual shift that is exhibited through Temple's library presents the best case for an urban site. The ASRS solution resolves the difficulty in balancing space for people, access to materials, and cost by keeping books on-site, available, and tightly packed. The balance between people and books in the library space is measured in book accessibility and retrieval time, which is now minutes instead of days, as was the standard at Paley. In addition, the operational costs run about 10 percent lower by eliminating the daily shuttling of books back and forth to an offsite location. These are practical considerations, but measured in relation to the inherent qualities of the creation of place. The Charles Library stores books but is more than a big book box. It contains people in places and offers moments of experience.

22

23

Functional Concerns – How the Space Works

The space-use needs of a research library are varied, but space is almost always at a premium. The demands on every square foot in the Charles Library are very high. Balancing the twin aims of future flexibility and versatility with current usability creates a tension between advocating for space that can be used in many ways and spaces that are highly specific. Well-proportioned spaces need to have appropriate ceiling heights for the size of the room, as well as adequate daylight and lighting control. They must be useful, interesting, and comfortable enough that a patron will want to stay for extended periods throughout the day, while also being flexible enough to be adaptable over longer timeframes as use and needs change. The top floor of Charles Library, for example, is daylit around the entire perimeter. (FIG. 22–23) Study areas for groups or individuals are comfortable and views of the surrounding areas make it a prime place to be on campus. The traditional reading rooms may remain of use for individual study, a core component of a university research library that is unlikely to change, but should they one day be obviated, their space can be adapted. The same holds for the stacks, which now dominate a portion of the space, but can be repurposed if another use supersedes browsing volumes. This kind of flexibility is very much needed in the current library setting. The rise of digitization and other ongoing cultural changes have presented challenges to the necessity of print as a medium. The vicissitudes of an age of great change require flexibility, not just day-to-day or event-to-event, but over longer spans of time. This approach of anticipating unforeseen change can be found in the planning and use of the digital scholars area where unknown future tools and future uses are a certainty. In the current iteration it is relatively flexible maker-space in the middle and seating on the perimeter, but this too can be reconfigured in the future.

Making Flexible Spaces

Within the public areas of the Charles Library a variety of spaces have been provided to accommodate library patrons: loud or quiet; large or small; hard or soft; open spaces and intimate niches; some designed to accommodate high traffic and some enclosed and hidden, and some spaces near collections. The Charles Library serves as a catalyst for learning and intellectual engagement, built on the conceptual model of library as a learning commons, a model that emerged in the beginning of the twenty-first century as new technologies in the library setting began to offer expanded opportunities for research and learning. In this model, Temple's Special Collections, Temple University Press, and academic partners like the Temple Writing Center play a prominent role and are located in strategic places to give them a presence within the library.

The Charles Library also includes a more recent inflection: the notion of the library as a studio. From the creation of intangible ideas to physical things, the library is a setting for expression and creation as well as exploration and inquiry. It includes individual spaces and study rooms for students throughout the building. Some spaces are designed to accommodate single students working alone while others are meant to support the needs of collaborative teams. Consultation rooms, graduate studios, work stations and rooms for media screening are located throughout the building, as are instructional spaces with flexible furniture, screens, whiteboards, and other equipment for small and large groups as well as varied teaching and learning styles. Collaboration rooms and breakout spaces include a range of technologies to support creative production. The illuminated manuscripts of the medieval library would find a parallel function on the third floor of the Charles Library, which houses the Digital Scholarship Center (DSC), an expansion of a smaller experimental space that began in the Paley Library basement. The DSC is a maker-space, housing 3-D printers, prototyping equipment, laser cutters, CNC machines, and a whole range of electronics equipment. It includes other tools for creative output

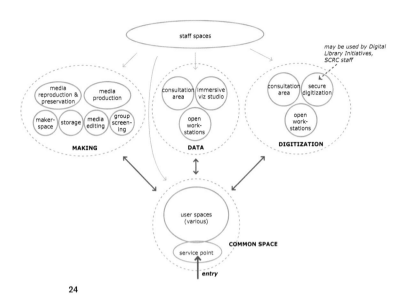

staff spaces

may be used by Digital
Library Initiatives,
SCRC staff

media
reproduction &
preservation

media
production

maker-
space

storage

media
editing

group
screen-
ing

MAKING

consultation
area

immersive
viz studio

open
work-
stations

DATA

consultation
area

secure
digitization

open
work-
stations

DIGITIZATION

user spaces
(various)

COMMON SPACE

service point

entry

24

such as gaming spaces and equipment, and media production areas. (FIG. 24) In juxtaposition to an environment long known as a place of knowledge consumption, research, and learning, the DSC offers students and faculty the ability to create, collaborate, and think through *making*. It is the only such space on campus not tied to any specific college or program.

How to Find What You Want in the Library

The most frequently asked question when the subject of the robotic book storage and retrieval system comes up is "What will it do to the serendipitous discovery of a book?" One can't wander around in the ASRS so the environment of discovery is digital and the user interface will need to find new avenues of exploration to mimic or replace traditional shelf browsing, ideally providing new paths to discovering content. The digital browsing environment is not restricted to only content that is in the physical books. As a global discovery environment, it may in some respects offer more than a traditional experience of looking for something in book stacks. It can seem like a devil's bargain when the trade offers the services of a robot in exchange for wandering limitless rows of books, and the nostalgic sense of loss is strong, but empirical data show that serendipitous discovery in book stacks is very rare. The problem of limited discovery can be addressed effectively, and offers something better than the results of wandering through close to two million books. Happening upon something useful online can be achieved using an algorithm that considers something a user is already looking at to anticipate what else might be of use to their research. There are options to show, for example, the spines of all the books that would be on the shelf of the book being considered, or ten other books of interest based on a topic. If desired, the whole group can be delivered as well.

The design of the library as a whole aims at an experience that is frictionless and easy to navigate. Users should be able to find the content, people, and services they are looking for. But the lifetime of the Charles Library is potentially one hundred years, so

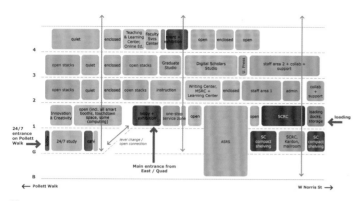

Image labels (in the diagram):

Floor 4: quiet | enclosed | Teaching & Learning Center, Online Ed. | Faculty Svcs Center | event + exhibition | open | enclosed | open

Floor 3: open stacks | quiet | enclosed | open stacks | Graduate Studio | Digital Scholars Studio | U. Press | staff area 2 + collab + support

Floor 2: open stacks | quiet | enclosed | open stacks | instruction | Writing Center, MSRC + Learning Center | enclosed | staff area 1 | admin | collab + support

Floor 1: Innovation & Creativity | open (incl. all smart booths, touchdown space, some computing) | lobby + exhibition | one-stop service zone | open | SCRC | loading docks, storage — loading

Floor G: 24/7 study | café | level change / open connection | ASRS | SC compact shelving | SCRC, Kardon, mailroom | SC compact shelving

24/7 entrance on Pollett Walk →

Main entrance from East / Quad

← Pollett Walk   W Norris St →

25

Programming phase diagram of functional adjacencies for the Charles Library.

the current generation will spend a very small amount of time in it when compared to future generations and the unforeseeable needs they will bring. Temple Libraries already has an enormous collection of electronic books and that number will grow exponentially over the coming decades. The ASRS will experience very little use if interaction with content becomes primarily digital. Perhaps one day, young people will come to the library on field trips and go up to the fourth floor to view a 40-pound book from the twentieth century with ornate illustrations, to examine it as a museum piece. The ASRS book storage area, as specialized as it is, was designed to anticipate uses other than book storage if that were desired in the future. Things may well change, perhaps dramatically so, and the issue of the ASRS and discovering content may not be as pressing or controversial an issue in the future.

Encouraging Innovation

The Charles Library is designed to encourage innovation in a variety of spaces by centralizing the services, by shifting the role of the staff, and by keeping a much greater percentage of space flexible, so people will always be able to use those spaces in ways that are serendipitous and creative. The variety of uses and spaces discoverable throughout the building suggest ways to wander through public areas. (FIG. 25) The diverse functions are appropriate for a learning commons and are able to both accommodate how people work now and encourage new and unanticipated modes of research, study, and knowledge production. By giving users more than they expected, perhaps the space itself can create a platform that encourages creativity, enables innovation, and helps those users accomplish more than they imagined possible.

The sustained success of the Charles Library's mission will be determined by its evolution over time in collaboration with its users. The building has a variety of spaces that offer different types of opportunities. In many cases the design objective was to simply create qualities of space that are good to inhabit, thereby allowing the best use of spaces to be determined by actual use and not by an organizational imposition. There are enough flexible spaces in the building that different arrangements can work for different users. In contrast, the Paley Library opened approximately fifty years ago and functioned more or less in a fixed manner for the whole of its existence as a library. The Charles Library is designed to have a different kind of horizon: it accommodates current functions without being overly prescriptive and therefore anticipates changes of use in the future.

Current use will be a determinant of many things, including the provision of furniture throughout the building. The occupation of the library in the summer of 2019 included plans for fixed uses in specific areas of the building, but a design process for a present-day research library cannot stop because the building has opened. Plans included analysis of specific user groups and assessment of space use. Library staff, for example, moved into a group workspace and were asked to analyze the change in use with the groups understanding that some adjustments would be made. Although there were decisions made about furniture and spatial configurations for research and study space, assessment of student use in the building over the first year determined furniture needs. The library purposely under-purchased a variety of types of furniture to see how they would be used in different spaces and how their use would in turn influence the uses of the space. Additional furniture will be purchased when use is more clearly established—the pieces that people gravitate to will be the ones that fill the spaces.

The design of the new library as a place that encourages and inspires, is flexible and inviting were important goals. Similarly to understanding particularities of behavior in relation to furniture, Temple Libraries has a goal of understanding the success of the library as a whole. Understanding if students feel more engaged in learning and want to be interactive with their peers and with new resources is important, but providing an enriching environment does not spontaneously translate into contributing to learning. Post-occupancy success for the library can be measured when varying degrees of use are understood. Studies of the success of user engagement in the library will be examined using three tiers. The bottom tier is utilization, which determines how often certain transactions and interactions are happening. Utilization is discovered through crude measurements and statistics, for instance, tallying the number of books checked out or how many questions are asked at the help desk. The middle tier of success is satisfaction, which is a more useful measure that requires inquiry and investigation. It asks if people are happy with the availability of materials, the usages of the space, the quality of support services, the tools and technology. Impact, the third tier of success, is the hardest to measure. This measurement seeks to discover how well the library has enabled the people who use it to achieve their purposes. It involves correlating when, for example, a user attends a library instruction session or has a consultation with the Writing Center and how they perform on a subsequent paper or a test.

As a piece of architecture, the Charles Library was designed and now stands as a building that offers welcome varieties of space, engagement, and inspiration. It was built to invite people in to research, to study, and to participate in the experience of learning and contributing to the collected knowledge of our past, present, and future. Great consideration was given to the making of place—to aligning function and character—and to creating a destination that will provide in experience what it promises in scale and form. The harmonization of presence and role is intended to exert an organizing influence over Temple's campus, and to make a statement, not only to the Temple campus, but also to the community, the city, and the broader academic world. How well the functions of a library work, how easy they are to identify, and whether they address the needs of library users go a long way in determining the library's success. The vision of the library as a place that both adapts to and anticipates growth and change over time gives it an important role in the university. This way of approaching design, especially for a library, accepts the vision of innovation as a central tenet of a university.

5

Charles Library
A Project Completed

Charles Library: A Project Completed

Charles Library: A Project Completed

Charles Library: A Project Completed

Charles Library: A Project Completed

153

157

Charles Library: A Project Completed

Charles Library: A Project Completed

Charles Library: A Project Completed

Charles Library: A Project Completed

Charles Library: A Project Completed

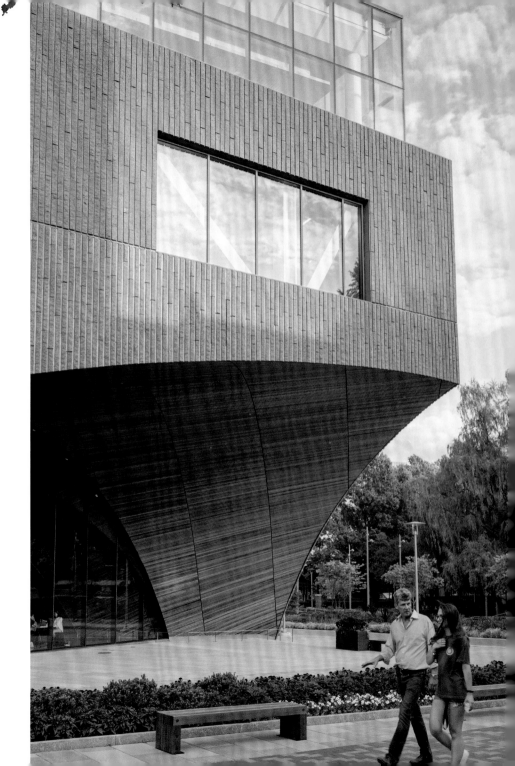

Charles Library: A Project Completed

Charles Library: A Project Completed

EVENTS

6

Civic Infrastructure
Campus, City, Culture

We designed the Great Room in the Library at Alexandria as a grand hall, after great libraries of the past: a very inspirational, unified space. You walk in and understand that anything is possible. It's also about society at large. Outside of the Great Room is a great public gathering place—the kind of public space that provides opportunity for a sense of communal ownership of a building.

Just prior to the Arab Spring, the Library at Alexandria had visitorship of nearly nine hundred people a day. Then the protests began. They were pretty severe—you could see buildings in flames just across the street, and I remember thinking, "Oh, my god, The Alexandria Library is going to burn down again." We watched as the Egyptian government collapsed. These were events for which the Library itself was partly responsible, because some of the first intellectual debates about regime change were held there. As the protests intensified, citizens of Alexandria formed a human chain around the library to protect it. In the end, not one item was taken from the building, nothing was destroyed, and everything continued to run. During the worst of the protests visitorship dropped to three hundred people per day until the government system changed. It's now back up to around five hundred visitors a day and climbing. Why did people protect the library, and what is bringing them back? The reasons are several, I'm sure, but I hope that the architecture has something to do with it.

CRAIG DYKERS
Snøhetta, March 6, 2016,
Campus, City, Culture Symposium,
Temple University.

Civic Infrastructure: Campus, City, Culture

1

2

Fundamentally, a library is a locus within a society that consecrates the process of learning and discovery. A library offers a place of physical participation in an enterprise that is at once both private and communal: inspiration and connection in the sanctum sanctorum of knowledge, progress, and enlightenment.

In a university setting, the library serves a symbolic role in addition to the practical one related to learning and discovery; if the young come to the university to experience an inner transformation that changes who and what they are, then libraries are the epicenter of that transformation. To communicate this sense, the Charles Library's fourth floor is a kind of embedded metaphor: the glass-enclosed space filled with light and with books brings the light of knowledge to the seeker who enters that space.

History of the Charles Library Project and Site

Early planning for a new library started in 2008 under the leadership of President Ann Weaver Hart, developed by the planning team and carried out by OLIN in collaboration with MGA Partners. The driving idea in the Temple 20/20 campus master plan was to focus development along Broad Street, a major north-south artery on the Temple campus's western limit. The one-hundred-foot-wide thoroughfare connects the center of Philadelphia with its northern neighborhoods and beyond, and it seemed to offer an opportunity for Temple to boost its presence and raise its profile in the city. Temple's signature buildings—Mitten Hall, Conwell and Carnell Halls, Rock Hall, and the Baptist Temple (now known as the Temple Performing Arts Center)—were built along Broad Street. However, for half a century development focused on the campus east of there, which has created a closely packed campus largely hidden from passing traffic. Temple University's public presence along Broad Street had become a chaotic and ad hoc segment between Cecil B. Moore Avenue and Diamond Street. The emphasis of Temple 20/20 was creating connections to Center City and making a respectable, dignified, and exciting space out of Broad Street. The original siting of the new library would have made it the first academic building on the

3

west side of Broad Street, serving as an anchor across the wide street and placing it in juxtaposition to buildings of architectural and historical significance, so that together they would serve as a gateway along the main north-south axis of the city. The urban relationship would fashion a symbolic entry declaring to the city the University's mission as an educational and research institution. Temple 20/20 would not be seen to its completion, but before it was superseded by a different plan it did produce Morgan Hall at Broad Street and Cecil B. Moore Avenue, south of the initial library site, a building which announces the intentions of the campus from its southernmost extent. (FIG. 3)

Snøhetta signed on in 2012 to design the library on the original Broad Street site, just before plans for the campus began to change direction. A new university administration brought with it new ideas about the University's role and the student experience on campus became a primary driver for campus planning. The new library, the centerpiece of the University's major development initiative, was to be moved eastward to support the student-centered planning initiative, but the density of the campus's built environment, created in part by the University's construction boom in the 1960s, meant a very limited number of options for the library location. The Temple 20/20 plan had designated an area where Barton Hall (now demolished) stood as future open space. When the new campus master plan, called Visualize Temple, was adopted in 2014 this site—located between Thirteenth Street, Liacouras Walk, Polett Walk and Norris Street—was designated as the site of the Charles Library. (FIG. 4) Snøhetta, along with the University planning team and other campus planning partners, came to understand that moving the new library east of Broad Street catalyzed a very powerful way of looking at the campus. Snøhetta worked closely with Temple to select a site by testing volumetric options as they related to the existing context. While the library site in the Temple 20/20 plan would have produced an eye-catching building on a main thoroughfare it would have done little to affect the main fabric of the campus. Relocating the library site through the Visualize Temple plan brought with it an opportunity to open up and give

4

order to the campus as a whole. The new central location of the library, coupled with the future demolition of both Beury Hall and the Biology-Life Sciences Building, allowed an opportunity to expand the open area around the Bell Tower, thereby creating a green quadrangle—a public commons—that creates an identifiable campus core. (**FIGS. 1-2**)

The library for the newly selected site would have to be a very different kind of building from the one that had been envisioned for Broad Street. To continue to ensure its urban importance and role as a symbol of the University, the library would still need to demonstrate the dignity and gravitas that was envisioned for Broad Street. However, since it was hemmed in by narrower streets and pedestrian walkways, and in close quarters with other campus buildings, the campus-enclosed site also required the library to be more personable. With heavy pedestrian traffic at the center of campus, the Charles Library is touched and engaged by people up close and from all sides. The location ensured that the Temple community would have an intimate relationship with the Charles Library both as a space to be in and as a distinct place on campus.

The library's re-siting raised another pressing issue. As planned for North Broad Street, the site clearly announced the University's intentions of a civic building project. The library was understood as being both for the University *and* for the North Philadelphia community. The Broad Street site promised to be an accessible and welcoming place for the community and the library was intended to provide a place the University could share with the community. Moving the library into the center of the campus, deep within its borders, shifted the relationship of the library and the community. Architectural gestures of invitation and openness would necessitate finding new ways to clearly invite the community onto campus so the library would still be a welcoming place for local residents. Conceptually, the Broad Street site was an announcement, a declaration of purpose and importance. The Thirteenth Street site is a call to come learn. Broad Street broadcasts; Thirteenth Street converses.

Despite this shift in priorities the Charles Library was still

5

6

planned to be monumental. It was to be an iconic building that stood out, large and robust. The size alone would be a statement of its importance. It is designed to command recognition and respect. At the same time, as an aspirational space the library was planned to have an engaging and inviting character. The library gains value as a place of the Temple community's collective accomplishments; its architecture can convey that sense. The Charles Library achieves this by clearly expressing that it supports Temple's mission as a research institution, while simultaneously extending an invitation indicating that it belongs to and serves *everybody*.

This understanding begins on the exterior. The inviting nature of the Charles Library originates with the view from a distance and continues as one enters. (FIG. 5) The architectural form makes it comprehensible and the transparency provides a sense of empowerment. The large arches, particularly the eastern-facing one, draw people into the main space. The entrance is glass and allows a view in from adjacent public spaces. Entry-level arches are easy to discern, and the large architectural gestures and lofty entry space, inscribed in the curvature of the forms, signal that something unique is happening inside. These architectonic features and forms are aspirational and uplifting, while also prioritizing vision and orientation as primary features of the library. The oculus at the top of the main arch grants a view all the way up to the fourth floor reading room. As such, from the main lobby you can see all the levels of the library at one time. Moving through the building brings the user to multiple, diverse spaces—from extremely lively to calm and refined. The navigation in the library is clear, allowing users to easily move between individual spaces and major areas of the building. This opening up of discernible, penetrable, and navigable space, in which users know where they are and how to get to where they want to go, allows for a sense of empowerment and mastery of the space.

While the active eastern edge of the library addresses the newly-constituted main open space on campus, the quieter western façade of the library, along Liacouras Walk, adheres to the uniform urban grid. There are two entries into the library on the western

7

8

9

on the western façade, one at the midpoint of the building and another at the southern corner. The southern portion of the wall offers glimpses into the corner café space on the ground floor and other work and study spaces on the upper floors. Meanwhile, the portion of the façade to the north of the entrance includes a solid exterior wall that encloses the ASRS. Despite being more enclosed than the eastern façade, the design for the western façade takes into account the need to keep Liacouras Walk active through the integration of architecture and landscape architecture. (FIG. 6) Snøhetta achieved this by utilizing the uninterrupted wall along the ASRS as a tranquil backdrop for the gardens that stretch along the western edge of the building, inviting people to gather in the layers of landscape punctuated with benches placed along the façade.

This approach to landscape is consistent with the larger ideas of green space developed in the Verdant Temple landscape master plan. (FIG. 10) The surrounding streets remain open to traffic while providing continuity with and supporting campus open spaces and gardens, streetscapes, and pedestrian walks. The quadrangle planned for the space east of the library provides the opportunity for Thirteenth Street to serve as a festival street, sometimes closed to vehicular traffic so people have the space for themselves. The library is suffused with, and surrounded by, a variety of scales, connections, and uses of public space. The scale of intimate gardens on the western edge along Liacouras Walk, the juncture of O'Connor Plaza and the smaller-scale Founder's Garden to the south, and the quadrangle to the east, are all connected and visible through the library's ground floor entry hall. The juxtaposition of scale in these garden spaces surrounding the library are important for the range of activities the spaces can support in the center of the campus (FIGS. 7–9).

In the 1960s Temple's growth was expansive and rapid to accommodate the increased number of post-war college students. The effect of a unified vision was a uniformity of buildings and an institution that projected an architecturally modest, albeit modernist, agenda. The neutral "background" buildings that comprise the majority of the Temple campus attest to the growth

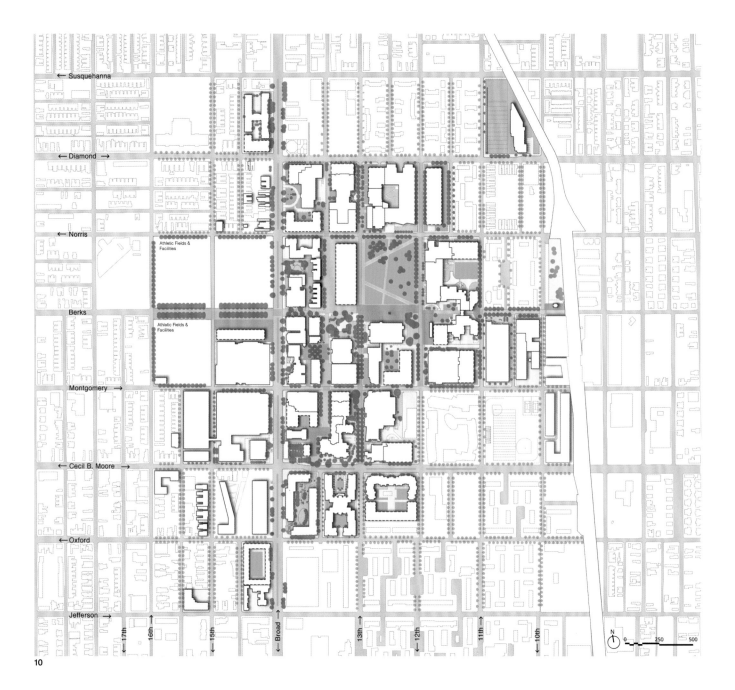

← Susquehanna

← Diamond →

← Norris

Athletic Fields & Facilities

Berks

Athletic Fields & Facilities

Montgomery →

← Cecil B. Moore →

← Oxford

Jefferson

17th 16th 15th Broad 13th 12th 11th 10th

N 0 250 500

10

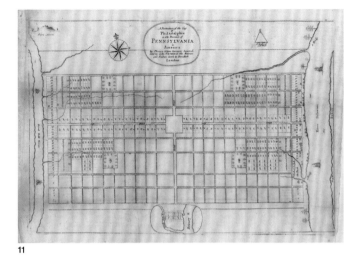

11

of an urban commuter campus. In the 1960s, they were designed and built to fill the grid and create a continuous context. They made sense as part of the uninterrupted fabric of the city, but within the construct of the campus environment, they do not convey a clear sense of hierarchy. As such, a visitor arriving at the main open space of the campus, the Bell Tower Plaza, would understand it as a center without providing any sense of arrival.

The Charles Library, an identifiable and architecturally ambitious building in the center of the campus, coupled with the future quadrangle, will offer something more than just an open area at the center of campus. The quadrangle and the library work *together*—like the Greek *stoa* and *agora*—to institute a new sense of scale on a scale-less campus, providing a proper sense of arrival at a distinct place. Thus, the context that has favored a neutral architecture set into the urban grid has accommodated something singular and prominent. This also links the new campus center with the lineage of the four public squares of the original plan of Philadelphia laid out by William Penn and Thomas Holme in 1683. The plan devised by Penn and Holme is a quincunx, with those city squares arranged around a central City Hall. (FIG. 11) The squares define Philadelphia and its commitment to open spaces as a community-shared amenity. They are part of the fabric and language of Philadelphia. In a campus setting, the quadrangle by the Charles Library will serve a similar function, offering a place of welcome and significance in a shared open space.

Bringing the library into the interior of the campus supports the notion of library as a place for all. The inviting gestures, the monumentality, size, and scale, all on display and given adequate room by the open quadrangle, allow the Charles Library to announce itself as a significant and organizing presence, a gesture that anticipates the future of the University. The library is designed to be a landmark, one that honors the past and serves as a good steward to the University's mission. Importantly, its monumentality and its welcoming qualities—human scale, transparency, and comprehensibility—work hand-in-hand with Temple's values of inclusivity and diversity. The Charles Library is a public place, a place that people want to be in, full of natural light and

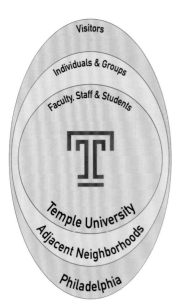

12

13

welcoming spaces. In part, the pull of the place is due to these extroverted and welcoming qualities, created by the affiliation of complementary aspects: monumentality along with affability, conveyed through architecture to express a sense of optimism and possibility.

An emphasis on accommodation and intelligibility is realized through use and access to services. The library as the university center can be understood in terms of concentric rings of community in the university setting. The internal core is the university community, the first ring includes individuals and groups in adjacent neighborhoods, and the outer ring consists of the larger city community. (FIG. 12) The sense of arrival on campus brings to light the opportunity for access and community building. The library's public event space, located prominently on the first floor and easily accessible from the main entry space, is a first encounter and a symbol of the library's openness and human-scale dimensions. (FIG. 13) Visible from Liacouras Walk, it provides a gesture of welcome to all who pass by. Active community outreach continues to be an important initiative for Temple Libraries; the welcoming design augments the idea of the Charles Library as a community destination. The sense of welcome and outreach is not only achieved architecturally, it is also supported by the services that are offered. The Charles Library's housing of the Urban Archives is key to this mission. The unique collection contains records of local news and community organizations from a more recent era, documents that together represent the everyday life and pace of the city and region in the nineteenth, twentieth, and twenty-first centuries. As part of Special Collections, the Urban Archive is valued by both scholarly researchers and private citizens alike. The resources are made available to a broad constituency serving Temple's commitment to community engagement. In the new library, the archives are given a prominent location on the main floor, strengthening the gesture of access and connection to the campus, neighborhood, and city communities.

The Charles Library is geographically located roughly in the center of four branches of the Free Library of Philadelphia—with the Lillian Marrero Library to the northeast, the Kensington

Civic Infrastructure: Campus, City, Culture

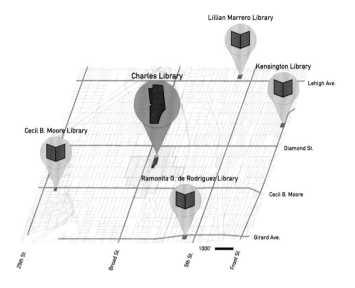

Lillian Marrero Library

Kensington Library

Charles Library

Lehigh Ave.

Cecil B. Moore Library

Diamond St.

Ramonita G. de Rodriguez Library

Cecil B. Moore

Girard Ave.

1000'

25th St.

Broad St.

5th St.

Front St.

14

Library to the east, the Ramonita G. de Rodriguez Library to the southeast, and the Cecil B. Moore Library to the west. (FIG. 14) But its success in connecting with and building community comes from the library's ability to complement the programming and collections of the nearby branches of the Free Library. The special collections and other services will play an important role in the Charles Library's role in engaging with the broader communities of the neighborhood and city. The services and collections that the Charles Library has to offer posit it as a partner with the potential to enhance access rather than repeat what is already available in the Free Library system.

A Library in the Digital Age

The contemporary library is a contested space. Debates about the place of physical media and traditional collections wage on, unsettled. The debates make the design of a library all the more poignant and interesting. But for the Charles Library, the role of media, collections, and content delivery are embedded in more fundamental core questions related to the role of the library. Questions that align with Temple University's identity and objectives include: the broader social function of a library, the value of the commons, the role the library plays in the continuity of social and cultural memory for Philadelphia, and the importance of a civic presence and the public good.

Centrally important to all of these topics is the purpose of a library facility, given that research can be separated from collaboration and engagement. The availability of digital resources and communication tools allows individuals to engage in research, scholarly work, and knowledge production in locations other than an academic library. Comparison of ideas and dialogue can be carried out from anywhere at any time, and collaborative production and making does not always require spatial adjacency. Given this, relevance of place requires that social engagement is well considered as an important factor in design; the reasons for being in a library must override the efficient and effective use of digital communication tools and materials for research.

15

16

The media of society's records have varied over time, but the primary goal of collections has not. Libraries continue to house social and cultural artifacts, the evidence of a society's memories and ideas. Even so, contact with tangible evidence through artifacts—collections and books in the stacks—is only a small part of the reason for a library, especially as collections and books are digitized and available in virtual form. In the ubiquitous knowledge and communication environment, therefore, the design of physical places becomes increasingly important. The role of serendipity and discovery that is treasured by library patrons can continue to be fostered through the design of physical space; materials and information can be deployed and accessible in a manner that makes spatial engagement meaningful. For the Charles Library, any discussion of the ASRS that houses almost two million densely-stored and unbrowseable volumes and cultural artifacts always raises questions of the loss of the library as a place. Many people consider any separation between a patron and a book repugnant, and only more so when introducing robots at a time of great anxiety over technology's perceived intrusions into a contested space freighted with nostalgic meaning. But storage is an ineluctable constraint and the Charles Library's prime location is a key factor in developing an active engagement with the community. The paradox that this presents guides and aids design: people, connecting with artifacts and other people, allow the social dimension of the library to connect with the cultural dimension. The Charles Library's configuration keeps books and collections close by and readily available. The flexibility of the library provides room for collections in juxtaposition to spaces for learning, making, collaboration, and debate. These functions exist alongside spaces for individual study and research within the library, an opportunity that surpasses the experience of a limited-use library. While research and engagement can occur from anywhere, the library of the present is a social space where research and engagement are greatly enhanced by community. (FIG. 15–19) This is the value of the library as learning commons and the root of the project's conceptual frame of the library as *stoa*, an archetypal model that has both formal and social impact.

17

18

19

As an urban project, the design of the Charles Library takes into consideration its contribution to the urban imagination as well as the urban fabric of the City of Philadelphia. Designed in parallel with campus plans—Temple 20/20, Visualize Temple, and the related Verdant Temple Landscape Master Plan—the library has served a prominent role in the University's future-focused campus and academic development. The library along with the landscape master plan serve as a way to stitch the campus into the urban, social, and cultural fabric of the City of Philadelphia, addressing the importance of the public good in both the physical and social dimension. The proposed quadrangle and the library together shift the scale of the University. By emplacing them firmly into the campus center, they form a new sense of arrival for visitors, and by extension, an identity for Temple within the city. The importance that Temple's focus on innovation and campus transformation plays in the city are well stated in a *Philadelphia Business Journal* article from 2015: "Temple's comprehensive campus plan, Visualize Temple, plans a large central green space, revamped library, and new interdisciplinary sciences building... Temple is revamping its crucial buildings on campus without expanding much beyond its current footprint."[1] The article also notes that the aim is to attract researchers to the University. As indicated in the article's title, the list includes fifty civic projects that are transformative, many of which, like the Temple campus work, are alterations that work with the Philadelphia urban fabric. And like the Charles Library, some are also planned to expand the City's capacity through facilities that are focused on innovation while adding to the urban infrastructure. Cited in the list are projects that accommodate the daily life of the city such as the completion of Dilworth Park at City Hall—which was visited by 10.8 million people in 2018, an increase of 24 percent since it was redeveloped by the Center City District[2]—and the development

1. Dan Norton, "Transformations: 50 things that will change Philadelphia in 2015," *Philadelphia Business Journal,* January 23, 2015, updated Feb 1, 2015. https://www.bizjournals.com/philadelphia/datacenter/transformations-50-thingsthat-will-change.html?page=all accessed March 6, 2019.
2. Levy, Paul, and Inquirer. "Dilworth Park's New Coffee Kiosk Benefits Philadelphians

20

redeveloped by the Center City District[2]—and the development of the Schuylkill Banks promenade in Center City—for 33,500 user trips per week.[3] Both of these projects are important interventions in the existing city fabric that have increased the capacity of the City's social infrastructure. Additional projects that add to the City's capacity for innovation and research include a new development plan for 30th Street Station, Drexel University's Innovation Neighborhood Plan, and the Pennovation Research Center at the University of Pennsylvania.

The Charles Library, together with these other urban infrastructure projects, presents a snapshot of a city moving into a new era where public space, access, and innovation-focused research are considered to be important contributions to civic identity and the infrastructure of a livable city. In a broad sense, these new urban endeavors connect with the psyche of Philadelphia where urban form and civic institutions have always been part and parcel of the making of the city. Philadelphia's iconic city plan is well recognized as part of the civic identity, but from its origins as a city, Philadelphia's civic institutions have worked in parallel with the plan to reflect the social dimension of the city. For example, public space in Philadelphia was conceived of as accessible to all citizens and public space continues to demonstrate an important civic value. **(FIG. 20)** Civic institutions like the Free Library also have an important social and cultural dimension; the Free Library continues to perform this role within Philadelphia, serving as an innovative leader among library systems by anticipating the social needs of those it serves and demonstrating their importance in library programming.

As Philadelphia develops and grows its social infrastructure and capacity for innovation and change, the cultural continuity of Philadelphia's early civic endeavors will continue through the

2. Levy, Paul, and Inquirer. "Dilworth Park's New Coffee Kiosk Benefits Philadelphians and the Future of Our Public Spaces | Opinion." Https://www.philly.com. February 27, 2019. Accessed March 27, 2019. https://www.philly.com/opinion/commentary/dilworth-park-starbucks-public-spaces-center-city-district-paul-levy-20190227.html.
3. "SRDC 2018 Annual Report." Schuylkill Banks – Plans & Reports. January 22, 2019. Accessed March 27, 2019. https://www.schuylkillbanks.org/plans-reports.

Civic Infrastructure: Campus, City, Culture

transformation and development of its institutions and public spaces. Temple's unique role as Philadelphia's public research university—with values such as access and diversity considered as important as innovation—gives it an important and significant ongoing role in the city's future that is a conscious effort to be both responsive to and reflective of the city's needs. The making of the Charles Library is Temple University's most recent responsive and reflective piece of urban infrastructure; the library adds to the City's continuity—spatially, socially, and culturally.

The Charles Library's extroverted form opens the building to its surroundings, encouraging collaboration, creativity, and innovation. It is a community building—the Temple community is a base that defines a core of the Temple campus and includes the larger communities of the neighborhood and city in concentric circles. From a campus perspective, the building provides a positive disruption within the urban fabric and has been a positive force in shifting the campus architecture and social spaces. Its purpose in the campus landscape is to serve as a connector—between buildings and open spaces, between faculty and students, between university and neighborhood, between Philadelphia and the world.

DOZIE IBEH
Associate Vice President, Project Delivery Group,
Temple University, Interview, October 2018.

7

Drawings

Site Plan

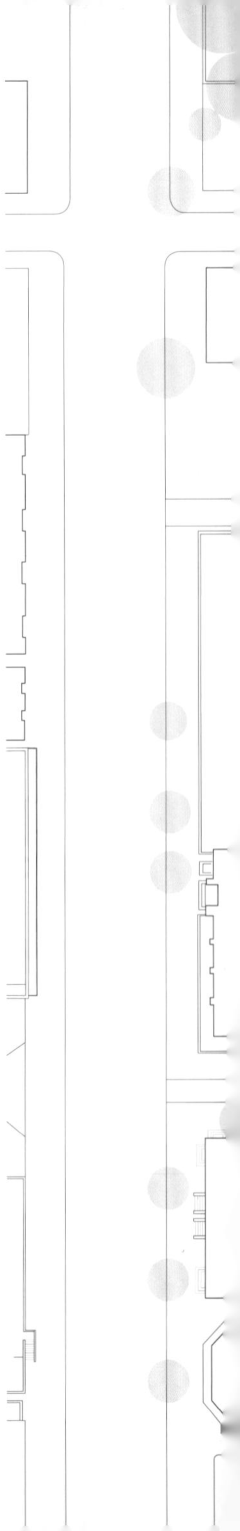

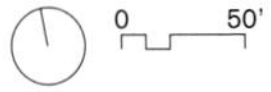

0   50'

Drawings

Norris St

Liacouras Walk

N 13th St

Polett Walk

Level 1

1. Lobby
2. 24/7 Lobby
3. Cafe
4. Event Space
5. One Stop Service Desk
6. Exhibition
7. Reading Room
8. Office
9. Book Bot

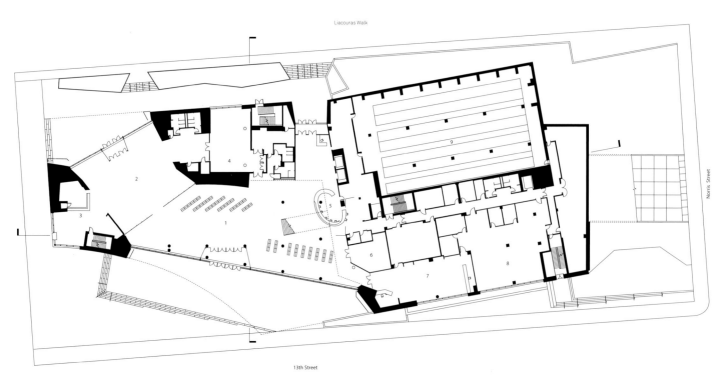

Drawings

Level 2

1. Instruction Room
2. Computer Lab
3. Writing Center
4. Offices
5. Book Bot

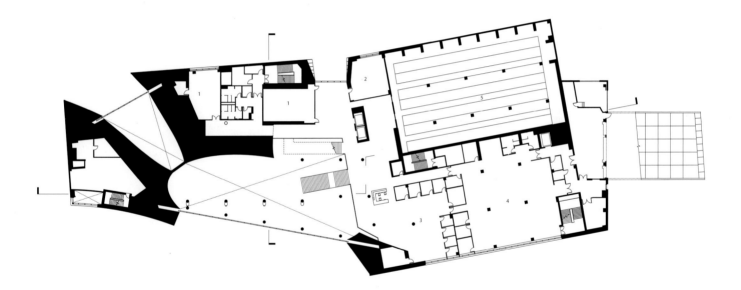

0   50'

Level 3

1. Scholars' Studio
2. Student Success Center
3. Reading Room
4. Offices
5. Staff Lounge

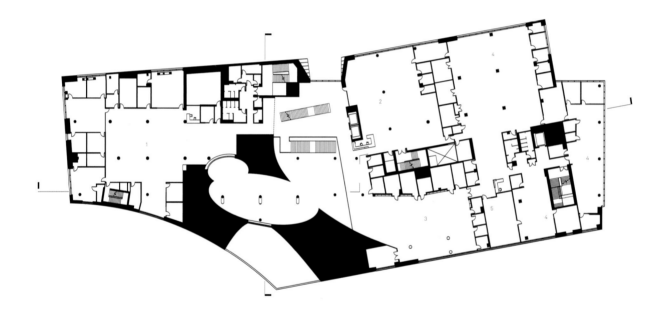

0   50'

Level 4

1. Reading Room
2. Browsable Collection
3. Oculus
4. Graduate and Faculty Studio
5. Green Roof

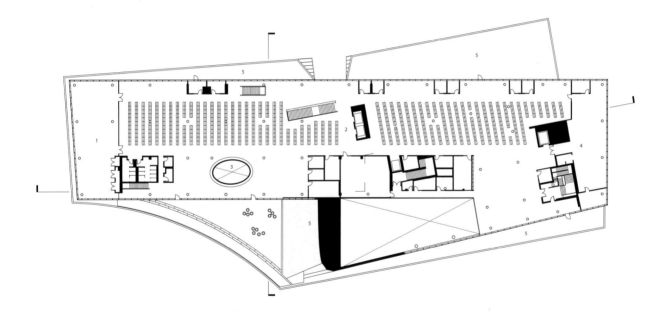

0   50'

North Elevation

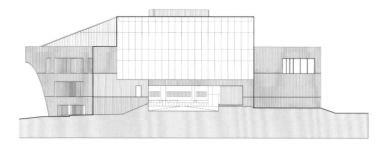

South Elevation

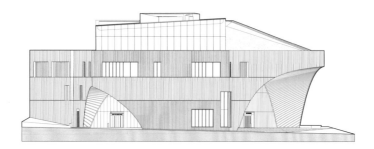

0   50'

West Elevation

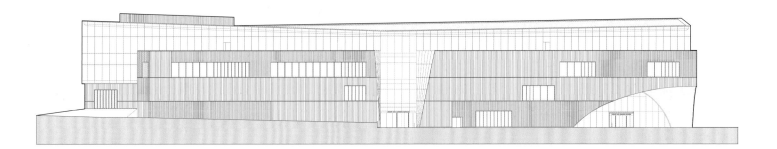

East Elevation

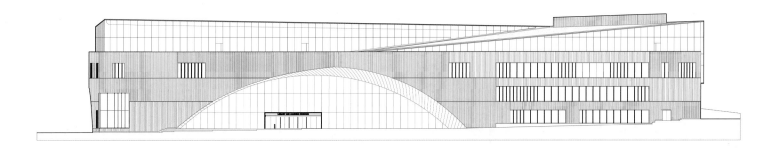

0   50'

Section Looking West

1. Lobby
2. ASRS
3. Classroom
4. Open Offices
5. Browsable Stacks
6. Reading Room

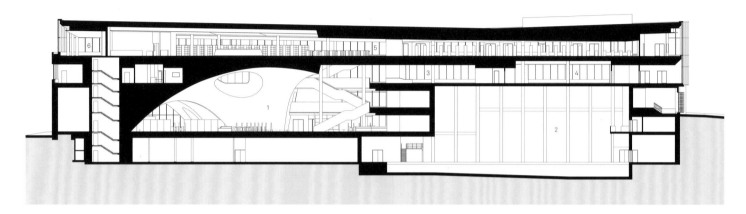

Section Looking North

1. Lobby
2. Oculus
3. Event Space
4. Browsable Collection

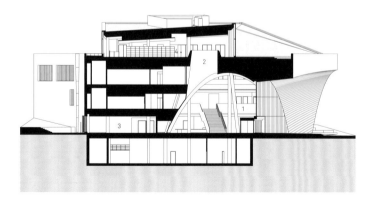

The curved framing for the cedar clad domes was constructed using a digital coordination process that allowed the contractor team to model and locate every element of the dome in a 3d model.

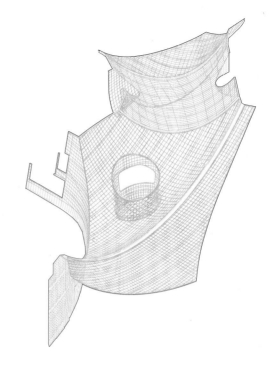

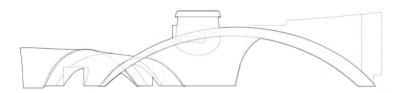

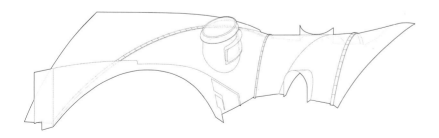

Afterword
The Early Life of the Charles Library

"What a school thinks about its library is a measure of what it feels about education."

HAROLD "DOC" HOWE II,
U.S. Commissioner of Education 1965-68

If the insight offered by Harold Howe II, the former Commissioner of Education, is true then Temple University is a school that places tremendous value on the education of its students. In the few short months since its inauguration, the Charles Library—designed by Snøhetta in association with Stantec—has been a sensational success. It has garnered admiration from the architectural press, being described as a "soaring ode to knowledge" and a "great accomplishment." But more important than the architectural plaudits is how quickly the library has insinuated itself into both the social life and physical context of the campus.

In its early days the library saw nearly 25,000 visitors come through its doors on a daily basis and it continues to serve an average of 7,000 people per day. At any given time the library is bursting with life—ranging from lively conversation amongst groups of friends in the ground-floor café to quiet contemplation over a book or laptop in the wide variety of reading rooms and study spaces. The Charles Library has quickly become the heartbeat of the university. As described by Temple University Provost JoAnne A. Epps at the building's opening ceremony, "We're going to meet at the Charles. We're going to have great ideas at the Charles. People are going to fall in love at the Charles."

The new library has given an immediate sense of gravitas to the center of Temple's campus. The adjacent public spaces, like O'Connor Plaza, have never felt so filled with activity as they have in recent months. The building's corduroy-like granite façade provides a backdrop to the surrounding life of the campus—creating a plethora of places to meet friends on the way to lunch or to simply take a short break between classes. Such is its impact that it is already difficult to remember what the campus was like without the library standing there at the intersection of

Polett and Liacouras Walks, welcoming visitors into the warm embrace of its rolling cedar archways and light-filled gathering spaces.

Architect Craig Dykers has described the library as a "generational project" that will have a long-lasting impact on the university. This will hold true in myriad ways. The many communities that are served by the library are only just beginning to discover the riches that it has to offer. Over time there is no doubt that library will be used by its communities in ways we can't begin to imagine today. Furthermore, the library's role as an organizing force of the larger campus will become clearer over the coming years as the university continues the project of reinventing itself through the creation of a campus quadrangle in front of the library's main entrance with the forthcoming demolition of Beury Hall and the Biology-Life Sciences Building. This long-term project will make a reality out of the vision of the Charles Library as both the crossroads and intellectual heart of the university.

Only time will tell just how impactful the Charles Library will be on the future of Temple University. But for the foreseeable future Temple students—as well as the broader communities across the campus and surrounding neighborhoods—should heed the wise advice of Ron Weasley in J.K. Rowling's Harry Potter and the Chamber of Secrets, "When in doubt, go to the library."

PHILLIP M. CROSBY
Adjunct Associate Professor
Tyler School of Art + Architecture, Temple University

Acknowledgments

Special thanks to Justin Coffin, William O'Neill Bourke, and Hayden Smith for their contributions in assembling the book and to the Temple University Libraries and the Tyler School of Art and Architecture for financial support for this project.

Project Credits

Design Architect, Landscape Architect, Interior Architecture: Snøhetta
Executive Architect: Snøhetta & Stantec
Architect of Record, Sustainability, LEED Consultant, and MEP Engineering: Stantec
Civil Engineer: Hunt Engineering
Structural Engineer: LERA

IT/AV: Sextant Group
Façade Consultant: Heintges
Green Roof Consultant: Roofmeadow
Lighting Consultant: Tillotson Lighting Design
Programming Consultant: brightspot strategy
ASRS/Bookbot: Dematic
Early Sitework and Deep Foundations Prime Contractor: D'Angelo Brothers, Inc.
Foundations and Waterproofing Prime Contractor: Hunter Roberts
Structural Steel Prime Contractor: Owen Steel
General Prime Contractor: Daniel J. Keating
Mechanical Prime Contractor: AT Chadwick
Plumbing/FP Prime Contractor: AT Chadwick, MK Fire Protection
Electrical Prime Contractor: EJ Electric
Low Voltage Prime Contractor: Atlantic Coast Communications
Moving Coordinator: Richard L Hoffman & Associates, Inc.
Mover: T&N Van Lines
Signage: Urban Sign and Crane
Furniture and Shelving Suppliers: Premier Office Solutions, Pomerantz, Moser
Furniture and Shelving Installers: RIFF and AIMM
Dome Geometry and Framing Fabricator (Sub to GC): RadiusTrack
Carpentry and Concrete (Sub to GC): Thomas Building Group
Masonry Contractor (sub to GC): Dan LePore and Sons
Glazer (Sub to GC): National Glass
Roofer/Green Roof (Sub to GC): EDA/G.R.A.S.S.
Testing and Inspections: Pennoni Associates and ATC Group Services
Commissioning Agent: Wright Commissioning
Smoke Control System Special Inspector: Bala Consulting Engineers, Inc.

Temple University
Project Delivery Group:
William Barnes
Margaret Carney (planning stages)
Michael Gentile
Dozie Ibeh
Julia Mullin
Alex Nichik
Sara Tice

Temple University
Library Staff:
Steven Bell
Richie Holland
Jonathan LeBreton (planning stages)
Joe Lucia
Marianne Moll
Margery Sly

Snøhetta Design Team:
Behrang Behin
Lauren Bordes
Chad Carpenter
Laia Celma
Jeffrey Cheung
Ian Colburn
Michelle Delk
Craig Dykers
Alan Gordon
Joyce Hanlon
Lara Kaufman
Douglas Kay
Nicholas Koster
Alex Krippner
Kurt Marsh
Jacqueline Martinez
Benjamin Matthews
Matthew McMahon
Nathan McRae
Karli Molter
Misako Murata
Anne-Rachel Schiffmann
Chen Sun

Stantec Design Team:
Anton Germishuizen
Scott Sullivan
Kristin Shiffert
Travis Byrne
Matthew Capelli
Tony Clifford
Marjorie Dona
Jessica Fisher
Jon Helhowski
Daniel Helmlinger
Kristy Hollis
Stefan Lesiuk
Greg Mick
Brennan Onushco
John Romano
Jill Sirota
Michael Thompson
Linda To

Book Design Team:
Pablo Mandel – book design
CircularStudio.com
Kirby Anderson – managing editor
ORO Editions

Image Credits

Unless otherwise stated, all drawings, model views, renderings, and photographs of projects designed by Snøhetta appear courtesy of Snøhetta. The following credits apply to all images for which separate acknowledgement is due.

Social and Cultural Memory: The Idea of Library:

Figure 1: Bibliotheque Sainte Geneviéve, Henri Labrouste, Architect, photo by Priscille Leroy from Wikimedia Commons, used under a Creative Commons License (CC BY-SA 4.0). https://commons. wikimedia.org/wiki/Biblioth%C3%A8que_Sainte-Genevi%C3%A8ve#/ media/File:Fa%C3%A7ade_de_la_Biblioth%C3%A8que_Sainte-Genevi%C3%A8ve,_sud-est.JPG

Figure 2: Bibliotheque Sainte Geneviéve, Henri Labrouste, Architect, photo by Marie-Lan Nguyen from Wikimedia Commons, used under a Creative Commons License (CC BY 2.0 FR). https://commons.wikimedia.org/wiki/ File:Salle_de_lecture_Bibliotheque_Sainte-Genevieve_n01.jpg

Figure 3 and 4: Paley Library, Nolen and Swinburne Architects, photo by Lawrence S. Williams, Special Collections Research Center, Temple University Libraries, Philadelphia, PA.

Figure 5: Paley Library, Nolen and Swinburne Architects, Special Collections Research Center, Temple University Libraries, Philadelphia, PA.

Figure 6: Fisher Fine Arts Library, Frank Furness Architect, United States Library of Congress Prints and Photographs Division, digital ID ppmsca.15371.

Figure 7: Van Pelt Library, Harbeson, Hough, Livingston and Larson Architects, photo by Daderot from Wikimedia Commons.

Figure 8: University of Pennsylvania Men's Dormitories, Cope and Stewardson Architects, United States Library of Congress Prints and Photographs Division, Digital ID HABS PA,51-PHILA,566B-4.

Figure 9: Princeton University Graduate College, Ralph Adams Cram Architect, Popular Science Monthly from Wikimedia Commons.

Figure 10: Cathedral of Learning, Charles Klauder Architect, photo by Alex Liivet from Wikimedia Commons, used under a Creative Commons License (CC BY-SA 2.0). https://commons.wikimedia.org/wiki/ File:Cathedral_of_Learning_blue_sk.jpg

Figure 11: Suzallo Library, Bebb and Gould Architects, photo by Robert Ashworth from Wikimedia Commons, used under a Creative Commons License (CC BY 2.0). https://commons.wikimedia.org/wiki/File:Suzzallo_ Library_at_UW_(9572958209).jpg

Figure 12: Sterling Memorial Library, James Gamble Rogers Architect, United States Library of Congress Prints and Photographs Division, digital ID highsm.19254.

Figure 13: Carnell and Conwell Halls, William Harold Lee Architect, photo by Robert Bauers, Special Collections Research Center, Temple University Libraries, Philadelphia, PA.

Figure 14: Temple of Learning, William Harold Lee Architect, Special Collections Research Center, Temple University Libraries, Philadelphia, PA.

Figure 15: Temple University campus main entrance gate, photo by Robert Dias, Special Collections Research Center, Temple University Libraries, Philadelphia, PA.

Figure 16: Temple University campus, Nolen and Swinburne Architects, Special Collections Research Center, Temple University Libraries, Philadelphia, PA.

Figure 17: Temple University campus plan, Nolen and Swinburne Architects, Office of Public Information, Special Collections Research Center, Temple University Libraries, Philadelphia, PA.

Figure 18: Paley Library entrance lobby, Nolen and Swinburne Architects, Lawrence S. Williams, Special Collections Research Center, Temple University Libraries, Philadelphia, PA.

Fig. 19: Rendering of future campus Quad, Copyright MIR & Snøhetta.

Figs. 20-25, 28, 29, 31: Copyright Snøhetta.

Figs. 26, 27, 30, 32, 33: Copyright Michael Grimm.

Figure 34: Joseph F. Wiedelman, Special Collections Research Center, Temple University Libraries, Philadelphia, PA.

Figure 35: John W. Mosley, Special Collections Research Center, Temple University Libraries, Philadelphia, PA.

Figure 36: Myron Davis Photography, Gray Panthers Photograph Collection, Special Collections Research Center, Temple University Libraries, Philadelphia, PA.

On Site: Construction Documentation:

All images by Betsy Manning, Temple University.

Community and Cultural Identity: Stories, Spaces, Functions:

Figure 1: Diagrams, range of library functions, library services, brightspot strategy.

Figures 2: Image by Dustin Fenstermacher for Temple University.

Figures 3, 4, 5: Images by Ryan Brandenberg, Temple University.

Figures 7, 8, 9, 11: Images by Joseph V. Labolito, Temple University

Figures 6, 10: Images by Betsy Manning, Temple University

Figure 12-13: Charles Library users ideal visit diagrams, brightspot strategy.

Figure 14: Charles Library services diagram, brightspot strategy.

Figure 15: Charles Library navigation, brightspot strategy.

Figure 16, 19, 22, 23: Copyright, Michael Grimm.

Figure 17: Paley Library study area, Special Collections Research Center, Temple University Libraries, Philadelphia, PA.

Figure 18: Charles Library ASRS book storage system, Betsy Manning, Temple University.

Figures 20, 21: Program space comparison, Charles and Paley libraries, brightspot strategy.

Figures 24-25: Diagrams, program distribution, brightspot strategy.

Charles Library: A Project Completed:

All images Copyright of Michael Grimm.